Totally WINTER

Edited By

Sherrill B. Flora

Publishers
T.S. Denison & Company, Inc.
Minneapolis, Minnesota 55431

Some of the material has been compiled from *The Preschool Papers* - September 1987 through Summer 1989, written by Sherrill B. Flora.

Standard Book Number: 513-01997-7
Totally Winter
Copyright © 1990 by the T.S. Denison and Company, Inc.
Minneapolis, Minnesota 55431

CONTENTS

*HOLIDAY AND SEASONAL UNITS FOR CHILDREN
AGED PRESCHOOL THROUGH GRADE TWO*

WINTER

— CONTENTS —

WINTER ART ACTIVITIES

WINTER WONDERLAND TREES

Follow the illustration next to this activity. Using green paper, draw a circle with a compass. Mark the center of the circle. From the center of the circle draw a straight line to the edge of the circle. The teacher will need to prepare the circles for younger children. First and second graders will enjoy using a compass.

The circle should be cut out and a cut made on the straight line. overlap the ends of the circle and staple at the bottom. The children can add glitter and small pieces of cotton to the trees. Arrange the trees on a table top, with a small sign saying, "Our Winter Wonderland." The table top arrangement can be made even more interesting when "little people" or people made by the children are added to the wonderland display.

SNOWFLAKE BALLOONS

You will need: white string, balloons, glitter and plaster of paris. Blow up enough balloons for every child in the class. Mix the paster of paris in a bowl. Dip the string in the plaster of paris and wrap around the balloons. When the plaster of paris is still wet, sprinkle the balloon and the strings with glitter.

When the plaster of paris is dry and hard, pop the balloons. The stings will hold the shape. The sparkling balloons can be hung from the ceiling.

WINTER NIGHT

Have the children create a "Winter Night" painting by using white paint on black construction paper. When the paintings are dry the children can add sticker stars to the night sky in their pictures. Older children may wish to add snow people to their pictures made from small cotton balls.

 # MY WINTER ACTIVITY LIST

Make a list of all the things that you enjoy doing during the winter season.

	Name
1.	- -
2.	- -
3.	- -
4.	- -
5.	- -
6.	- -
7.	- -
8.	- -
9.	- -
10.	- -

This is a good activity for two children to work on together.

LET'S MAKE FROST

Fill a shiny tin can with ice and salt. What do you think will happen to the outside of the can? Frost will form on the can. The temperature of the outside of the can is below the freezing point. The water vapor contacts the outside of the can and it changes directly to ice crystals or frost.

FEED THE BIRDS

During the long and cold winter months many birds will appreciate our help in providing them with some extra food. By creating classroom bird feeders, you are also providing the children with a wonderful experience of observing nature. Be sure to tell the children the real names of the birds and something about their feeding habits. Here are some fun ideas for creating classroom bird feeders:

• Fill an ordinary mesh bag (like the bags that oranges come in) with suet. Hang in a tree. Chickadees can hold onto the bag as they eat!

• Wrap chicken wire around a large piece of suet and hang in a tree.

• Melt lard or suet. Put bird seed in a paper cup (almost full). Pour enough melted lard over the seeds to stick them together. Stir. Put a string in the center to hang with. Put the cup in the freezer until very hard, then tear off the paper cup and hang in a tree.

ICE CUBE POPS

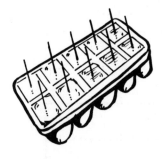

Fill an ice cube tray with fruit juice or a powdered drink mix such as Kool-Aid. Put a popsicle stick or plastic toothpick in each section of the ice cube tray. Freeze the ice cube tray in a freezer, or the tray can be left outside to be frozen. Older children may enjoy timing how long it takes for the juice to freeze. This is an easy and fun snack idea for the children.

Let's Go On A Sleigh Ride To Grandma's House

Name

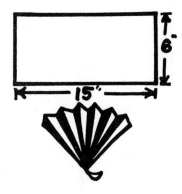

NORTH WIND

During January the cold north wind blows! Here are some fun experiments using the concept of wind.

Fan: Cut standard 12" x 15" paper *(drawing paper preferably)* in half lenghwise; allow the children to decorate and fold into a fan. *(See illustration.)*

Let's Make Wind: The children make wind by fanning themselves, shelves, curtains, mobiles, hanging objects.

Demonstrate wind drying: Draw two squares of the same size on the blackboard. Wet both. Fan one, notice that it is drying faster than the other.

From these experiences the children should develop an understanding that:

- Air is all around us.
- Wind is moving air.
- Wind can do work, turn windmills, move sailboats, dry clothes, fly kites, etc.
- Wind can hold things up such as kites and gliders.
- Wind makes waves in the water.
- Wind can be harmful (storms).

NUT SNACK

Here is a fun, healthy treat that children really enjoy! Stir peanuts, raisins, pretzels, and various dry cereal in a large bowl and serve in paper cups. Adding small marshmallows or M&M's can add an extra fun surprise in each paper cup treat.

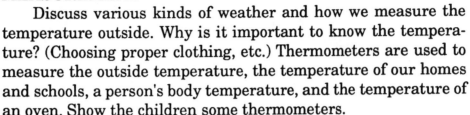

MEASUREMENT

Discuss various kinds of weather and how we measure the temperature outside. Why is it important to know the temperature? (Choosing proper clothing, etc.) Thermometers are used to measure the outside temperature, the temperature of our homes and schools, a person's body temperature, and the temperature of an oven. Show the children some thermometers.

What other kinds of measuring tools are there? Rulers, measuring cups, measuring spoons, yardsticks, measuring tape, weight scales, etc. Let the children experiment with various kinds of measuring tools. Let the children use scales and rulers to measure different things. Encourage the use of vocabulary words such as: longer, shorter, heavier, lighter, taller, empty, full, etc. Place a weather thermometer outside your classroom and check the temperature daily.

WINTER SAFETY

Dramatize winter safety situations. After a child dramatizes a situation, the class should decide if it is safe or unsafe. Here are some suggestions for the dramatizations: sliding near trees throwing snowballs at cars or people, skating on a pond, climbing on large snow piles. Which are safe? Which are not safe? How could some of the situations be made safe?

MAGNIFYING GLASS SNOWFLAKES

Snowflakes are beautiful to look at. It is difficult to imagine that all snowflakes are different. Children are fascinated by looking at snowflakes under a magnifying glass. After examining the snowflakes, let the children draw a picture of a snowflake, using white chalk on blue or black paper.

SLIDING IN THE WINTER

Slide down the hills with your pencil. Don't fall off the hill!

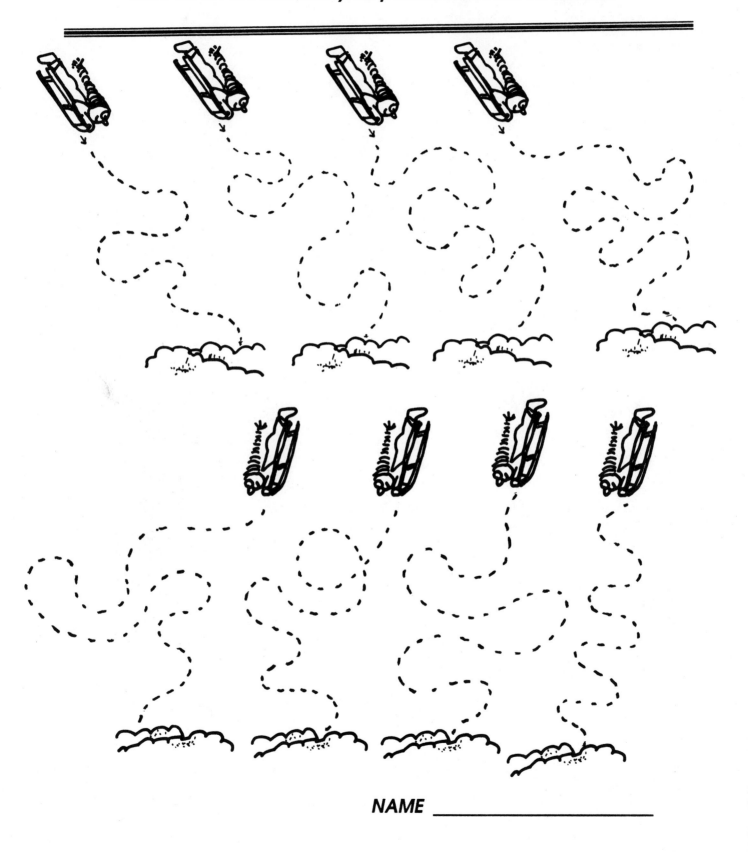

NAME _____

WINTER FINGER PLAYS/RHYMES

FIVE LITTLE SNOWMEN
Five little snowmen, happy and gay.
First one said, "What a beautiful day."
Second one said, "We'll never have tears."
Third one said, "We'll stay for years."
Fourth one said, "But what will happen in May?"
Fifth one said, "Look! We're melting away!"
(This is a fun rhyme for the children to dramatize. Experiment with the word "melt." Provide the children with some experiences of watching snow or ice melt. Use as a flannel board rhyme. Patterns are included.)

A Melting Snowman
(make 1)

Snowman
(Make 4)

WINTER FINGER PLAYS/RHYMES

LITTLE BIRDS OF WINTER
Little birds of winter,
Sitting on the bough.
You are cold and hungry,
I will feed you now.

Here are crumbs and raisins,
You will like, I know.
Come and eat your breakfast,
On the fresh, white snow.

*(Use as a flannel board rhyme.
Patterns are included.)*

WINTER FINGER PLAYS/RHYMES

TEN LITTLE SNOWMEN
(May be sung to the tune of "Ten Little Indians")

One little, two little, three little snowmen,
(Extend three fingers, one at a time)
Four little, five little, six little snowmen.
(Extend three more fingers, one at a time)
Seven little, eight little, nine little snowmen,
(Extend three more fingers, one at a time)
Ten little snowmen bright.
(Extend tenth finger)

Ten little, nine little, eight little snowmen,
(Bend down three fingers, one at a time)
Seven little, six little, five little snowmen.
(Bend down three fingers, one at a time)
Four little, three little, two little snowmen,
(Bend down three fingers, one at a time)
One little snowman bright.
(Bend down last finger)

WINTER FINGER PLAYS/RHYMES

WINTER ACTION PLAY

Down the hill on sleds we go	*Hands held high together, slanted.*
Slide - Slide - Slide!	*Bring hands down - sliding motion.*
Across the field of crusty snow	*Hands together, palms down at left.*
Glide - Glide - Glide!	*Glide to right.*
Making snowballs, small and round	*Roll hands together.*
Throw - Throw - Throw!	*Throwing motion.*
Roll them down along the ground	*Bend down. Hand moves along ground as if rolling something*
Grow - Grow - Grow!	*Hands cupped together. Move widely apart slowly.*
Three big snowballs - Push and roll	*Hand next to ground - pushing then rolling motion.*
Pile - Pile - Pile!	*Hand palm down about a foot from the ground - bring up to higher position - then higher than self.*
Dot Mr. Snowman's mouth with coal	*Dotting motions with thumb and first finger - make wide smile shape.*
Smile - Smile - Smile!	
Silver blades upon the ice	
Skate - Skate - Skate!	*Skating motions with feet.*
Around the pond, once or twice	*Make wide circle with arm, twice.*
Try a figure eight!	*Hand makes figure eight in air.*
Someone's calling - Time to go	*Cup hand behind ear.*
Come - Come - Come!	*Beckon.*
Spice cookies and hot cocoa	
Yum - Yum - Yum!	*Rub stomach - smile.*

JACKY FROST

Oh, I think Jacky Frost
   is a strange little elf.
And I guess no one's seen him,
   not even myself.
But I know that he comes
   on the cold winter night.
And paints on our windows
   most beautiful sights.

When I see Jacky Frost
   I will tell him it's queer
That he never paints pictures
   when summer is here.
For I've looked many times,
   but there's nothing to see.
Don't you think Jacky Frost
   is as strange as can be?

*(Have the children draw pictures of what they think
Jacky Frost might look like. Older children may
wish to write a story about Jacky Frost.)*

Name _____

THE TALKING SNOW LADY

"Wow!" said Nick and Katie, "This is the best Snow Lady that we have ever made! She has a wonderful face."

Katie squealed, "Look Nick, her face is so real that she almost looks like she might talk to us."

"Oh Katie," said Nick, "I thought I saw her mouth move!"

Then, all of a sudden, the Snow Lady opened her mouth and said to Nick and Katie . . .

_____

_____

_____

_____

_____

_____

_____

_____

The children may wish to use this story starter as a creative dramatics experience. The children can play the roles of Nick, Katie and the Snow Lady. How many different stories can you think of?

OUTSIDE BUBBLES

Bubbles are a favorite of young children. Bubbles are fun and can be educational. Even though it is January, take the children outside to blow bubbles. Talk about which bubbles are large, which bubbles are small; which bubbles are big, which bubbles are little; which bubbles lasted a long time and which bubbles lasted a short time. How many bubbles can the children count? Older children can time the bubbles with a stop watch.

THE SNOWFALL GAME

Snow makes whiteness where it falls,
The bushes look like popcorn balls.
The places where I used to play,
Look like somewhere else today!

Review the poem with the children. Tell the children that we could have a snowfall in part of our room. Establish boundaries. After discussing how softly snow falls, have three children pretend to be snowflakes and turn into snowballs. Three other children walk around the room questioning where the old play area has gone under the snow. Discuss how the children felt as they came down as snowflakes. Ask the children who searched for the play area how they felt. (New vocabulary words - confused, mixed-up) Repeat the poem.

A fun art project: is to make a snow scene by using popped popcorn.

Practice Printing: This is a nice poem for the children to print. Have the children illustrate the peom.

WINTER MOVEMENT GAMES

JACK FROST FREEZE TAG

This is a typical game of "freeze tag," with the added fun of "Jack Frost." The person who is "it" is Jack Frost. Jack chases the other players in the game. When Jack Frost catches someone, Jack must touch their nose and "freeze" the person.

All the children should have the opportunity of playing the part of Jack Frost. Let each child "catch and freeze" several children. In this game of tag everyone has a turn so no one can lose.

MITTEN SCRAMBLE

Use the children's mittens. Have each child put one mitten on their hand and throw the other mitten into a pile. On the teacher's signal the children should scramble to find their matching mitten.

Variation: Half the children put on one of their mittens. The teacher should collect the remaining mittens and pass them out to the other half of the children. On the teacher's signal, the children should walk around the room and find the person who is wearing the matching mitten.

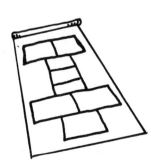

SNOWFLAKE HOPSCOTCH

Hopscotch can be an indoor game. Use masking tape on the floor to make the hopscotch chart or use an old discarded window shade. A hopscotch chart can be drawn on the window shade in permanent magic marker.

Let the children take turns "hopping" on the hopscotch chart. Each time that a child completes hopping, give the child a paper snowflake or a doily as a reward. Remember ... hopping within squares for a young child can be difficult. Every child should earn a snowflake. Trying is as important as mastering a skill.

Glitter Snowflake

Using white glue let the children outline the snowflake and add glitter.

Name _____

A Winter Story

A WINTER DAY

*(The children can pantomime the activities or create their own winter day fun. Emphasize the **BOLD** words as you read the story to the children.)*

Tim and Jim were sleeping in their warm beds when the alarm rang. The children **popped** their heads up, **rubbed** their eyes and **yawned**. They **stood up** and **stretched; standing on their tip toes** they **reached up.** Then they **bent over** and **touched their toes.** Mother was calling them for breakfast so Tim and Jim hurried. First they **put on their shirts** and **buttoned** them carefully. Next came the **pants, socks,** and **shoes.** The boys **raced** into the bathroom to **brush their teeth** and **comb their hair.** Tim and Jim **scampered down the stairs** and **sat down** at the kitchen table to **eat** hot cereal and **drink** orange juice.

It had snowed six inches the night before, so quickly the boys **put on their boots, coats, stocking caps, scarves,** and **mittens** and out the door they **went.** The snow was so deep the boys had to **pick their feet up high as they marched.** They decided to go sledding so Tim and Jim **ran** to the nearest hill, **dragging their sleds** behind them. The boys reached the hill and **sat down** on the sled. What fun they had as they flew down the slope! Tim **fell off** and hit a bump. He **got up** and **shook off all the snow** from his clothes. After sledding most of the morning, the children **skipped** home to get their skates.

It was a long walk to the ice pond because Jim stopped to **lay down** in the snow and **spread his arms and legs** to make snow angels. Tim **picked up** some snow, **packing it hard** in his mittens to **throw** at a nearby tree.

The pond was crowded but the boys had fun **skating around and around.** Watch out! **Down they both went!** Carefully they **tried to help each other up. Jim pulled Tim back down** on the slippery ice and **Tim held Jim down.** Finally they **slowly crawled on hands and knees** to the side of the pond, and **steadying** their skates on the snow, they **raised the rest of their bodies up.** After all this Tim and Jim were cold, so they **skated** to the warming benches to sit by the fire. They **rubbed their hands together** and **patted their arms** to stop from **shivering.**

Slowly the boys **untied** their skates and began **marching** home. As they entered the house they **stomped** the snow and ice from their boots, **pulled off wet mittens, hats, scarves,** and **unbuttoned their coats.** They **hung** everything up to dry. Tim and Jim **sat** in front of a crackling fireplace to warm themselves and **drink** hot chocolate. It had been a busy winter day!

From, Fun With Action Stories, by Joan Daniels.
Copyright © T.S. Denison & Co., Inc.

SNOWFLAKES IN THE SKY

Cover the background of the bulletin board with blue paper to represent the sky. Have the children make snowflakes to fill the sky. Here is an easy snowflake idea: purchase paper napkins that come folded in squares. Fold one point across to meet the other point. The napkin will now be a triangle. Fold the triangle in two again. Let the children cut on all three sides of the napkin. Carefully unfold, and a beautiful snowflake will appear. Place the snowflakes on the blue background. Add white cotton or quilt batting for clouds.

WINTER MUSIC ACTIVITIES

WINTER'S BIRTHDAY CAKE

One day the winter birds and squirrels decided to have a birthday party for a little wild rabbit who lived in the woods near them. They went to work and gathered acorns, pieces of bark and some wild berries that were still on the bushes. How they wished they had a birthday cake for the bunny, but no one seemed to know just how to make one. They went to bed that night a little disappointed, but while they slept... something happened!

My song will tell you what the surprise was.

Win-ter baked a birth-day cake With frost-ing deep and white. The cand-les were the i - ci - cles Gath-ered in the win-ter night.

Suggestion: *When you sing the song, show with your hands how deep the frosting was and put your fingers up like candles.*

COASTING

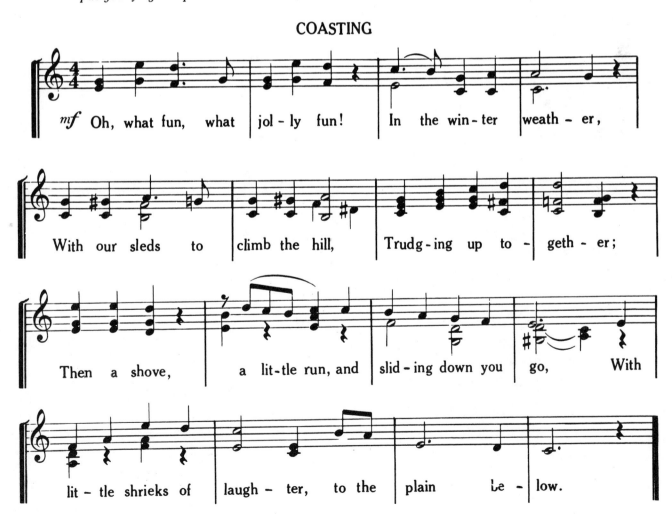

mf Oh, what fun, what jol - ly fun! In the win-ter weath - er,

With our sleds to climb the hill, Trudg-ing up to - geth - er;

Then a shove, a lit-tle run, and slid-ing down you go, With

lit - tle shrieks of laugh — ter, to the plain be - low.

WINTER MUSIC ACTIVITIES

A DAY TO SKI

If you were going skiing, what kind of day would you like to have? What kind of hill would you choose? What does the boy in the song talk about?

Suggestions: To the rhythm of the song, make your hands walk straight out in front of you as though on skis. Ski to the rhythm of this song.

The ground is white. The sun is bright. A love-ly day to ski!

I know where to go and find The ver - y hill for me.

WALKING THROUGH THE SNOW

Walking through the snow,
Deep, deep snow,
Way above my shoetops,
Everywhere I go!

Walking through the snow,
Deep, deep snow,
If I try to run at all,
Down I go!

Suggestion: Walk to the rhythm of the peom.
Lift knnes high. Fall down at the end.

Suggested Reading List

Hasler, Eveline. **Winter Magic.** Morrow. Copyright © 1984. *Summary:*
Peters cat takes him out into a snow covered world to show him the
secrets of winter.

Keats, Ezra Jack. **The Snowy Day.** Viking. Copyright © 1962. *Summary:*
The adventures of a little boy on a snowy day in a big city.

Lenski, Lois. **I Like Winter.** Walck. Copyright © 1950. *Summary:* A poem
telling what a child likes about winter.

Parnall, Peter. **Alfalfa Hill.** Doubleday. Copyright © 1975. *Summary:*
Describes the coming of winter and its affects on the animals.

Stevenson, James. **Howard.** Greenwillow Books. Copyright © 1980.
Summary: Howard misses the annual migration so he must spend winter
in New York City.

Thesselt, Alvin. **White Snow, Bright Snow.** Lothrop. Copyright © 1947.
Summary: When it begins to look, feel and smell like snow, everyone
prepares for winter.

Yolen, Jane. **Owl Moon.** Phillomel Books. Copyright © 1987. *Summary:* On
a winter's night under a full moon a father and daughter trek into the
woods to see the Great Horned Owl.

CHRISTMAS

CONTENTS

HOLIDAY TRADITIONS
AROUND THE WORLD

The following are some 'Around the World' examples of how other people celebrate during the Christmas Season.

WHO IS SANTA CLAUS?

In the United States Santa Claus is the man who comes down our chimney on Christmas Eve and leaves all those gifts that the children have asked for. Children in other countries call "Santa Claus" by different names.

DUTCH children call him St. Nicholas. St. Nicholas has a long white beard and is dressed in a bishop's robe. He comes on December 6th, St. Nicholas Eve. On that evening children leave out their shoes filled with straw, hay or carrots for St. Nicholas' horse. In the morning they find that he has left them a present, usually a toy gingerbread.

In SWEDEN, a small elf called Yulltomte takes the place of Santa Claus. He works in secret, remaining hidden under the floor boards. The work of Christmas would never get done without him. The children place a dish of rice pudding on the floor before they go to bed on Yule Eve. The children in Sweden also celebrate St. Lucy's Day. A girl wearing a crown of pine boughs and seven lighted candles awakens the family and serves them cake and coffee. On Christmas the white-bearded elf brings gifts.

In ENGLAND and AUSTRIA the children call Santa Claus "Father Christmas," and in FRANCE he is called Papa Noel.

WHY DO WE PUT TINSEL ON THE CHRISTMAS TREE?

Years ago, it is told, there lived a very good woman who lovingly cared for her large family. Every year the good woman would work very hard trimming the family Christmas Tree and trying to make Christmas as wonderful as possible for her family. One year, on Christmas Eve, after the family was asleep, many spiders crawled up the tree and spun many webs all around the tree. When the good woman awoke the next morning, she discovered that all the spider webs had been transformed into shining silver. It is said that this was the woman's reward for having been so good and loving.

Holiday Traditions
Around The World

THE CHRISTMAS TREE -
IS IT DIFFERENT IN OTHER COUNTRIES?

The Chinese call their Christmas Tree, the Tree of Life. It is decorated with paper flowers, colored paper chains, paper bells and cotton snowflakes. Wouldn't this make a beautiful classroom tree?

Years ago in England, on the afternoon of the day before Christmas would come the ocassion of uprooting a fir tree. The fir tree would be planted in the large Christmas tub and brought into the corner of the living room. The same tree would be used for many years and often would become a member of the family.

WHAT IS MISTLE TOE?

Kissing under the mistle toe came to us from Britain and the origins of the custom is unknown. The traditional form of the custom was that each time a kiss was claimed under the bough the young men picked off a berry. When all the berries were gone there was no more kissing.

A WONDERFUL CHRISTMAS GAME

After Christmas, when most families today are watching the television, the families of the Middle-Ages would be dashing around playing Christmas games. Besides the fun of playing these games together, the games would also settle the large Christmas dinner. In Normandy, over 70 years ago, between courses, everyone would stand up, hold hands, and dance around and around the table singing, *"En sacant! En sascant!"* a translation would be "put it in the sack! Put it in the sack!" (Sounds more fun than watching television!)

FRUITCAKE (EVEN CHILDREN WILL LIKE!)

1/2 cup golden raisins; 1/4 cup grape juice; 1 package vanilla pudding and pie filling; 2 cups milk; 1 tsp vanilla; 1 and 1/2 cups flaked coconut; maraschino cherries halved, pecan halves, 3/4 cup dry almond macaroon crumbs; 1/2 cup coarsely chopped pecans; 1/2 cup sliced pitted dates; 3/4 heavy whipped cream.

Soak raisins overnight. Combine pudding mix and milk in a saucepan. Cook and stir over medium heat until mixture comes to a full boil. Remove from heat. Add vanilla and coconut. Cool. Oil a 1 and 1/2 quart loaf pan lightly. Arrange maraschino cherry halves and pecan halves on the bottom of the pan. Fold raisins, nuts, dates, and macaroon crumbs into cooled pudding. Then fold in whipped cream. Spoon mixture over the cherries and pecans. Freeze 8 hours.

CHRISTMAS CREATIVE DRAMATICS

December is a time of joyous celebrations! Hanukkah and Christmas are two holidays that children love! *(Probably in part to all the gift giving!)* The following is a springboard idea for you. Whether you celebrate Hanukkah or Christmas you should be able to adapt the following ideas to your classroom's needs.

Dramatize a story using the following costume descriptions and illustrations. It is up to your imagination and the imagination of your children to create the story. The costumes would be appropriate for a trip to the North Pole to see Santa, or a visit to an old-fashioned toy-maker's shop, or what might happen after hours in the toy department of a large department store. Be creative - Plan your own production! Pick and choose from the following costume ideas.

Santa Claus - Form a tube of crepe paper to fit the child's head. Tie at the top. Decorate with cotton. Staple on a paper beard that has been covered with cotton.

Reindeer - Measure a brown construction paper headband to fit the child's head. Cut out and staple antlers to the sides of the headband. Wear wrist bells.

Jack-in-the Box - Decorate a large cardboard box, using white wrapping paper and colorful cut-outs. Leave the cover on the box, but cut out the back section. Dress a child like a clown. The Jack-in-the-Box jumps up when someone opens the lid.

Teddy Bears - Make a tube of black crepe paper to fit the child's head. Tie or tape the top. Cut out a semi-circle large enough for the child's face. Turn inside out. Staple a strip of yarn at the back of the neck and tie the cap around the neck to hold it in place. Add construction paper ears.

Wooden Soldiers - Make construction paper hats as shown in the illustration.

Rocking Horses - Yarn may be used as a mane. Crepe paper can be wrapped around the child's hands and feet for hooves. The child can rock back and forth on hands and knees.

Dolls - The girls wear party dresses and tie big bows in their hair. Pin a narrow ribbon on the back of the dress. Pretend to pull the ribbon to make the doll talk.

Spinning Top - Wear leotards and a crepe paper "tutu."

Cars, Trains, Trucks - Decorate a large cardboard box with construction paper wheels, doors and windows. Children can sit in the vehicles and pretend to be the toy drivers.

Name _____

The children decorate the tree
by using crayons, markers,
stickers, sequins and glitter.

Decorate
A Tree

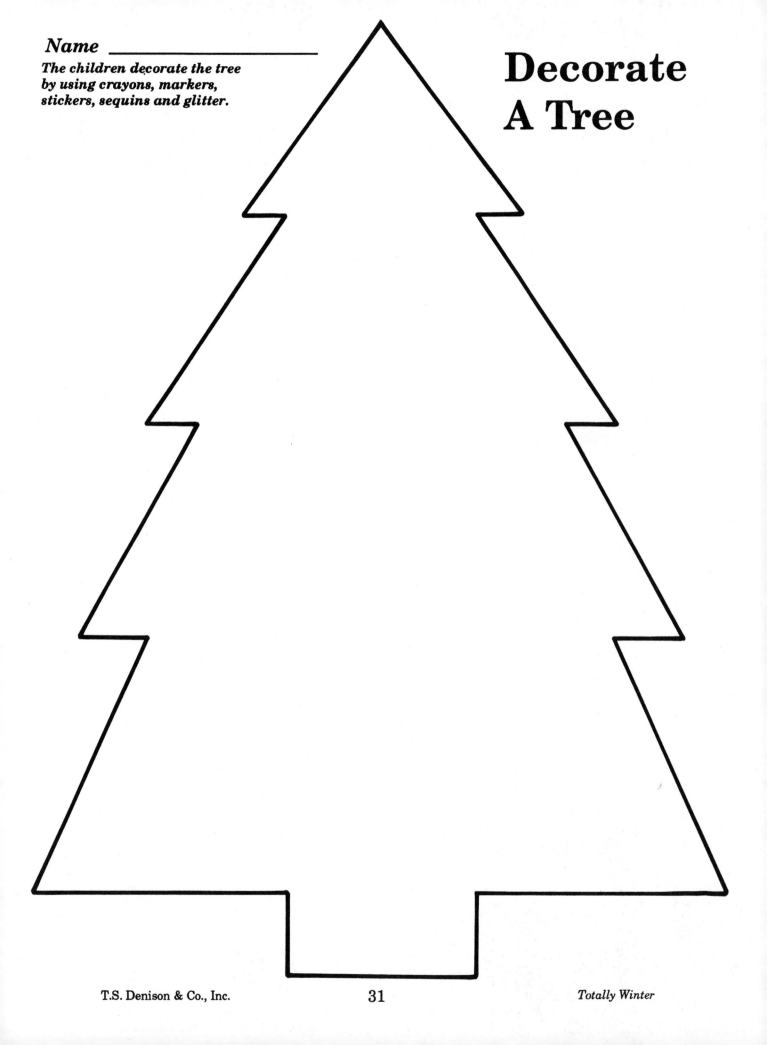

A CHRISTMAS STORY

SANTA CLAUS AND HIS CAT

It was Christmas Eve. Santa Claus had just finished all of the toys and was ready to go to the children, so he put on his coat and his cap and his mittens, threw his bag over his shoulder, opened the door, and looked out, and there was the great round sun shining as bright as day. Santa Claus laughed at himself and said, "Mercy, I can't go down to the children now; it is broad daylight and they would see me, and I must not let the children see Santa Claus."

So he put the blankets on his reindeer and went into the house. The great fire was burning brightly and Santa Claus's big armchair was in front of the fire looking so comfortable that Santa Claus said, "I will sit down and rest a bit."

Then he thought to himself, "I must be careful and not go to sleep." So he took his magic curtain and hung it up in the window. "Now," said Santa Claus, "when the sun goes down and the stars come out, if I am asleep, you can drop down and wake me."

So the curtain promised and Santa Claus sat down in his chair. He was so warm and comfortable that the first thing you know the sun went down and the stars came out, and the curtain dropped down with a bang (clap hands), but Santa Claus never heard it; he just slept and slept and slept.

Now Santa Claus had a little cat which was sitting by the fire. She looked up and there were the stars peeping in. "Oh," said the cat, "what shall I do? How will I wake up Santa Claus?"

Upon the shelf was a round brass plate and the kitty ran upon the shelf and knocked it down on the floor. It went bang on the floor, but Santa Claus never heard it. He just slept and slept and slept. And what do you think that kitty did? She climbed up in Santa Claus's lap and put her claws in Santa Claus's long white beard and gave one pull.

Santa Claus sat up with a start and looked in the window. There were stars shining and there lay the curtain on the floor. "Mercy!" said Santa Claus, "I will be late."

So he put on his coat, hat and mittens, threw his bag over his shoulder, banged the door, jumped into the sleigh, and away they went to all the children. And, if it hadn't been for that cat, there wouldn't have been any Christmas things for the children at all that year.

From Story Telling with the Flannel Board, Book Two.
Copyright © T.S. Denison & Co., Inc.

(Turn this story into a flannel board story. Patterns found on pages 33 & 34.)

STORY PATTERNS

(Patterns for Santa Claus and His Cat. Story found on page 32.)

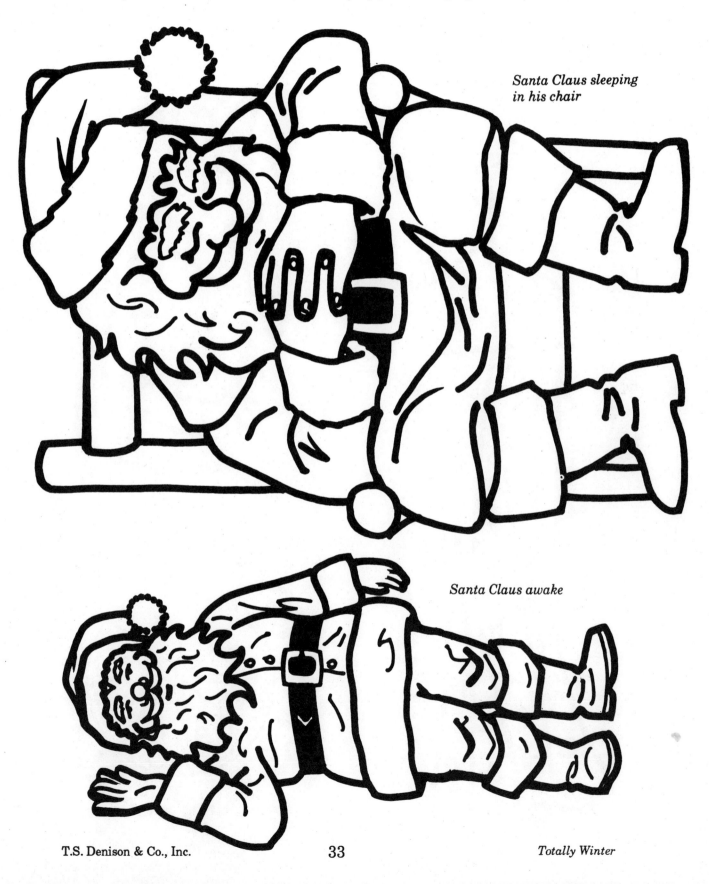

Santa Claus sleeping in his chair

Santa Claus awake

STORY PATTERNS

(Patterns for Santa Claus and His Cat. Story found on page 32.)

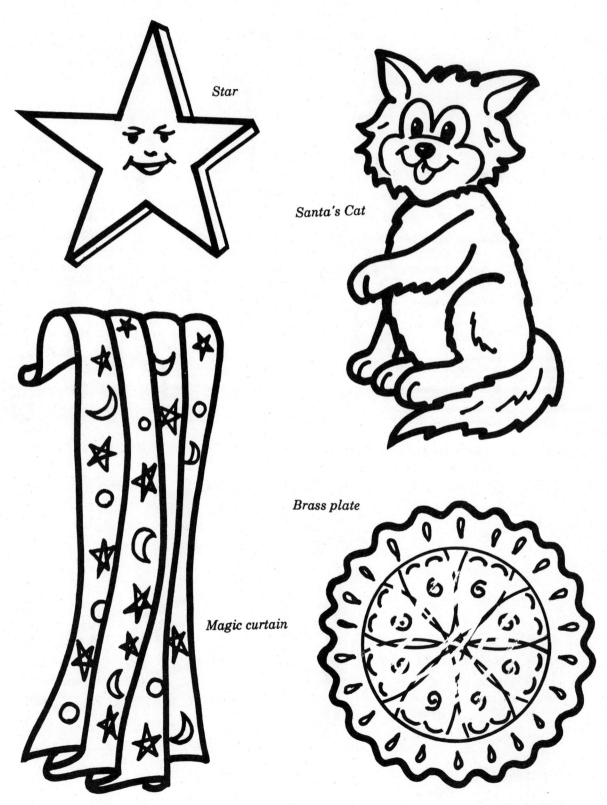

Star

Santa's Cat

Brass plate

Magic curtain

PEDRO'S CHRISTMAS FLOWER

"How are you this morning, Mama?" Pedro spoke softly as he bent over the thin white-faced woman who lay on the cot.

"Better, maybe - a little better, Pedro," she whispered. "Perhaps I can get up soon - maybe amnana, Pedro."

But Pedro knew it was not so. Each day his tired mother grew thinner and paler. If only he could have a good doctor come to the little adobe hut. If only there was medicine for her. But medicine cost money and Pedro earned hardly enough for food from the sale of firewood.

Pedro sighed as he closed the door. Today he must buy beans and if there was enough money left, a small piece of meat. How could he buy a Christmas present for his mother! But alas, that could never be.

Pedro placed the saddle baskets on each side of the little brown burro and led him out of the shed.

He walked behind the donkey. Now and then Pedro would stop to pick up a piece of dried mesquite or a piece of dead cactus. These he loaded into his baskets. But wood was hard to find in the desert. He walked farther than he had ever gone before.

He climbed a little rise of ground and stood looking down into the little valley below. A tiny stream trickled from a small rocky cliff. It ran into a little pool. Beside the pool, growing close to the water, were some tall pretty red flowers. Their leaves were glossy green. They shone like the wax candles in the church. Pedro ran down the slope to the flowers.

"They're beautiful," he cried. "Like - like Christmas. I'll pick Mama a bouquet for a Christmas surprise." He bent down and picked a beautiful red blossom. But almost as soon as he pulled the stalk from it's root, it withered. It's petals seemed to shiver and fade. The white sap dripped onto his fingers.

"Oh," Pedro cried, "They bleed. They die! But perhaps if I dig up the roots, too, they will keep for Mama's Christmas." He took a sharp stick and dug carefully about the roots. Soon he had a soft ball of earth with the red flower standing proudly upright in the middle. Pedro put the plant in the corner of one of his wood baskets. Then he kept gathering firewood. When the baskets were full, he turned the little burro back toward home. It was still early when he stopped at the house of his first customer.

"Buenos dias," Senora Martinez greeted him, "What a lovely flower you have there Pedro!"

A CHRISTMAS STORY CONTINUED
PEDRO'S CHRISTMAS FLOWER

"A beautiful flower," said a man who was standing beside the donkey. He was a stranger and had difficulty speaking the language. "It is for my Mama," Pedro said. "It is for ier Christmas."

"Dr. Poinsett is a great lover of flowers," Senora Martinez said. "At home in the United States he has a greenhouse where he raises many flowers."

"But that one," the tall doctor said, "is a new one to me. It is very lovely. Would you sell it, boy?"

"It is for my Mama," said Pedro. Then quickly, "But, if you are a doctor, perhaps you could help me, sir. My Mama is very sick and there is no doctor. If you would come, sir, I could show you where these flowers grow. You could have all that you want."

"You say your mother is ill?" The doctor had forgotten the flower.

"Oh yes, and white and thin. I try to help her, but she needsmedicine."

"I will come," said the doctor.

The good doctor got his black bag and Pedro led the way to the adobe hut. Pedro waited outside while the doctor made his examination. "Good food and the right medicine will cure her. You and I will go to the village and get what she needs. She is very sick now, but she will get better soon."

"Oh, Dr. Poinsett," cried Pedro, "you mean she will be well and strong again?"

"Yes," said the doctor, "but she will need fruit and vegetables. Beans are not enough. Come, we will go shopping." They went to the village and the good doctor bought fruit, vegetables, meat and milk. "You must eat these good foods, too, Pedro," said the doctor. "I will bring some each day while I'm staying with Senora Martinez. Then I will leave money for you to buy more good food."

"Graacias, gracias," cried Pedro. He prepared the food for dinner and hurried to wash away the dishes. Then he put the basket on the burro and hurried away to the little valley. The sun was going down before he finished digging out the roots of a beautiful red flower like the one he had dug for his mother. He took it to the good doctor. "Here is your Christmas flower," said Pedro.

"It will be the Christmas flower of many people," said the doctor. "Just wait and we shall see."

"It shall be my poinsettia flower," said Pedro. "I shall name it for you. You are making my mother well and we shall have a good Christmas."

"Poinsettia is a good name," said the doctor. "we shall call it that." So Pedro's red flower became the Christmas flower, not only to one nation, but to many. It is raised all over the country from which it came. Scarcely a cottage in Mexico is without its tall red flowers that almost cover the house at Christmas time. Pedro's flower is truly a great gift.

(Use as a flannel board story. Patterns found on pages 37 & 38)

From Story Telling with the Flannel Board, Book One,
by Paul S. Anderson.
Copyright © T.S. Denison & Co., Inc.

STORY PATTERNS

(Patterns for, "Pedro's Christmas Flower," found on pages 35 & 36.)

STORY PATTERNS

(Patterns for, "Pedro's Christmas Flower," found on pages 35 & 36.)

CHRISTMAS ART ACTIVITIES

CHRISTMAS STOCKING

This Christmas stocking is sometimes a challenge for very young children to make. The teacher needs to provide two stocking patterns for each child. The children cut out the patterns. The teacher holds the two patterns together and the child uses a paper punch, and punches out the holes around the stocking. The children can then sew up their stockings with yarn. Children can print their names on their stockings and decorate with glitter.

The teacher should hang up the stockings in the classroom. It is fun during the holiday party for the teacher to leave a surprise in the stockings (stickers, a fun snack, gum, etc.)

HOLIDAY ORNAMENT

This is a good gift idea. Cut cardboard rings from a large roll, such as a carpet roll. Paint the rings gold. Put a piece of pipecleaner through the top of the ring and form a hook, at the top and bottom of the pipecleaner. Mount a photograph of each child on a piece of colored construction paper. Put a string through the picture and hang it inside the ring.

CHRISTMAS TREE DECORATION

Using play-dough or homemade clay, have the children pat a piece into a pancake shape. Using a Christmas cookie cutter they can cut out a design. Some sequins or glitter may be used for decorating. A string is pressed in the back for a hanger. Place the ornaments in a windowsill or on paper towels and allow a week or two for drying. Here is a good recipe for homemade clay:

Recipe for clay: 1 cup flour; 1 cup salt; 1 tablespoon alum. Water mixed with food coloring is added gradually until the mixture is right. (No cooking!)

CHRISTMAS CANDLES

Children can make their own Christmas candles by using a cardboard cone and a little imagination. Empty thread cones used by commercial sewers are available at local recycling centers, or the teacher can make cones by using heavy construction paper.

The children should paint the cones white. Each child should be given a pattern or a pre-cut green construction paper leaf. Decorate the leaf with glitter. Glue the white cone on the center of the leaf. Add red tissue paper or cellophane flame in the top.

(from L. Lenahan, Springfield, MA)

CHRISTMAS ART ACTIVITIES

BELLS

Each child will need to bring from home an empty quart plastic bottle (pop or soda bottle). The teacherd will need to have small round tree ornaments, thin wire, aluminum foil, red rick-rack, glue, cutting tool and red ribbon.

Cut off the top bell-shaped portion of the plastic bottle. Remove the caps and punch a hole in the center of each. Replace the caps and cover the entire plastic bell with aluminum foil. Glue a row of red rick-rack around the lower edge of the bell. Thread a small round ornament on a piece of wire about seven inches long. Put a loop in the wire four inches from the round ornament to keep the ball in place after it is inserted in the bell. Insert the wire in the bell through the hole in the cap and make a loop at the top. Tie a red ribbon at the top of the bell.

MACARONI TREE

Give each child a cardboard cone. Have the children glue rows of shell macaroni around the cone until it is completely covered. When the glue has dried, spray the macaroni trees with gold spray paint. Glitter may also be added once the paint is dry.

CHRISTMAS GIFTS

Children love to make gifts for their parents. This is a traditional gift that all parents expect to receive at some point during their child's early years.

You will need: Pot pie pans, "Pam" no-stick spray, plaster of paris and poster paint.

What you do: Spray the pot pie pans with "Pam" no-stick spray. Mix the plaster and pour it one inch deep in the pans. Have the children make a handprint. When dry, unmold and have the children decorate their handprints with poster paint.

MY OWN DECORATED TREE.

You may wish to use the patttern found on page 31. Make the tree out of green construction paper. Provide the children with a wide variety of materials that can be used for decorating the tree; shells, glitter, sequins, popcorn, buttons, tissue paper, foil, etc.

Who will you give a gift to?
What will you give them?

CHRISTMAS RECIPES

GINGERBREAD

     1 package gingerbread mix
     1/4 cup water

Mix water and gingerbread mix. Refrigerate for at least one hour. Roll 1/8" thin. Bake at 375° for 6 to 8 minutes. Makes 3 dozen cookies.

KRISPY BARS

     Here's a fun snack: *What you need:* 3-quart saucepan; measuring cups; stirring spoon; square cake pan; 1/4 cup butter or margarine; 6-10 ounces marshmallows; 5 cups "Rice Krispoes."

     What you do: Melt the butter or margarine in a saucepan, add marshmallows and cook over low heat until marshmallows are melted and mixture is syrupy. Remove from heat. Add Rice Krispies" and stir until well-coated. Pour into buttered pan. Cool.

GRAHAM CRACKER COOKIES

     1 small package instant chocolate pudding
     1 and 1/2 cups milk
     1/2 cup peanut butter
     24 graham crackers

Mix peanut butter and milk. Add instant pudding. Let stand for five minutes. Spread on 12 graham crackers. Top with other graham crackers. Freeze (or eat unfrozen). Makes twelve.

SPECIAL GRANOLA COOKIES

     1/2 cup honey
     1 cup powdered milk
     1 cup peanut butter
     granola cereal

Mix honey, powdered milk and peanut butter together. Roll into balls and roll in granola cereal. Makes 2 dozen balls.

CHRISTMAS LEARNING GAMES

WRAPPED PRESENTS

Place felt pictures of wrapped presents on the flannel board. The presents should be in a variety of shapes; squares, rectangles, circles, etc. Point to one of the presents, naming the shape of the present. Ask the children to find another present that is the same shape.

Variation for older children: using the pictures of wrapped presents ask the children to draw a picture of what they think is inside the present or have the children write a short story describing what the present is, who it is for and who it is from.

HOW MANY DAYS

How many days until Christmas? A good way to answer and to show a child is to make a Santa Calendar. Draw a December calendar and fill in the dates. Put a Santa picture or sticker on the 25th day. The child will color one block each day until they see Santa's picture. The child can count each day after they color to know how many days until Christmas.

This activity can also be done for the eight days of Hanukkah.
(from Mrs. A. Miller, Kannapolis, NC)

WRAPPING PAPER LOTO

Use Christmas or Hanukkah wrapping paper or fabric for this activity. Cut several pieces of chipboard so that each measure 9" x 9". Cut material squares with a pinking shears (so it will not unravel) to a measure of 2" x 2". Use a variety of materials and cut two squares of each material. Glue one of each of the two alike squares on the chipboards. Put nine different squares on each board. Each board will be different. The second square of each material used will remain as a swatch for the teacher or leader.

This is how you play: Give a board to each child playing the game. The teacher or leader holds up one 2" x 2" swatch at a time. If a child has material on his/her board exactly like the one being held up, he/she takes it and places it on top of the matching fabric. The game is played until everyone has matched all the fabric on his or her board.

Name ⎯⎯⎯⎯⎯⎯⎯⎯⎯

Can you draw some toys in Santa's bag?

CHRISTMAS MOVEMENT GAMES

SANTA'S FOOTPRINTS

Mastering the concepts of left/right is a skill not achieved by many preschoolers. Although the concept may not be achieved , it certainly can be introduced during the preschool years. Most children at the kindergarten level begin to understand the concept of right/left, but sometimes even a first grader needs some reminding. The following activity is a fun one for working on the concepts of left/right. To make this activity seasonal, you can tell the children that they are following Santa's footprints.

From carpet padding, cut the four basic shapes - rectangle, square, circle, triangle. The shapes should be large enough for one or more children to walk around. Paint red footsteps around the outside edge. A child chants, "Right foot, right foot," as he puts his foot in the print and marches around. On the back of the padding, paint opposite footprints blue. Print L, and have the children chant, "left foot, left foot." Several children may march at the same time and play "Follow the Leader."

Variation: You can use construction paper cut-outs of foot prints. Tape the footprints in a maze in the classroom or gym and have the children follow the footprints. Older children may enjoy having to perform a task in connection with following the maze. Fill a basket with a variety of tasks (spelling words, science questions, gross motor skills, etc.) On several of the footprints print the word TASK. When a child steps on the TASK footprint the child must then pick a task from the basket.

TOY CHARADES

When children are waiting for the Christmas holiday or the Hanukkah holiday to begin, their little minds are often filled with thoughts of toys. Playing "toy charades" can be a lot of fun at this time of the year.

The children should all be seated in a circle. The teacher chooses one child at a time to "pantomime" or act out a type of toy that the teacher has whispered in the child's ear. All the children try to guess what type of toy is being pantomimed.

CHRISTMAS MOVEMENT GAMES

REINDEER, REINDEER, RUDOLPH

This game is to be played the same way that children play "Duck, Duck, Grey Duck." To keep with the "December Holiday" theme, children enjoy changing the "ducks" into "reindeers." During December it is much more fun to be chosen to be Rudolph rather than a Grey Duck.

GALLOPING REINDEERS

This activity is especially fun when you provide background music in a galloping tempo (4/4 time), but it is not necessary.

Introduce this activity to the children by saying, "Today let's be galloping reindeers. Watch and I will show you how to gallop." The children will watch at first and then try. Start by slowly galloping. Gradually speed up the tempo until all the children are able to smoothly develop a natural galloping gait.

You can create some extra fun by adding the directions of galloping fast to loud music and galloping slow to soft music. As you change the volume of the music the children will need to listen and pay attention in order to change the speed of their galloping.

SANTA SAYS

Children love imitating and playing "following directions" games. Instead of playing "Simon Says," try playing "Santa Says." Give the children directions to follow such as:
- Put your hands ABOVE your head.
- Put your hands BELOW your head.
- Put one foot UP.
- Put one hand ON your stomach.
- Put your RIGHT hand on your LEFT ear. *(older children)*
- Stand on your RIGHT foot. *(for older children)*

Name _____

Christmas Word Hunt

```
C  O  O  K  I  E  S  W  Y  G
H  Q  C  X  H  A  J  O  T  I
R  E  I  N  D  E  E  R  S  F
I  X  D  Y  L  F  L  V  L  T
S  A  N  T  A  O  F  Q  E  H
T  Z  F  R  M  M  U  S  I  C
M  B  R  E  G  P  K  I  G  X
A  R  B  E  L  L  S  N  H  D
S  N  O  W  T  Q  P  G  V  J
```

Read all the words in the "Word Bank." Find and circle all the words in the puzzle.

HOLIDAY WORD BANK

CHRISTMAS	**COOKIES**	**MUSIC**
SANTA	**SLEIGH**	**SING**
ELF	**TREE**	**GIFT**
REINDEERS	**BELLS**	**SNOW**

CHRISTMAS FINGER PLAYS/POETRY

SANTA'S REINDEER

Santa's little reindeer standing in a row	*(raise five fingers)*
When Santa comes they bow just so	*(bend hand)*
Then they fly to the left	*(move hand to the left)*
Then they fly to the right	*(move hand to the right)*
Then Santa's little reindeer sleep all night.	*(put hands behind your back)*

RING THE BELLS

*(Can be sung to the tune of
"Row, Row, Row Your Boat")*
Ring, ring, ring the bells.
Ring them loud and clear.
To tell the children everywhere,
That Christmas time is here!

TEN LITTLE REINDEER

*(Can be sung to the tune of "One Little,
Two Little, Three Little Indians")*
One little, two little, three little reindeer.
Four little, five little, six little reindeer.
Seven little, eight little, nine little reindeer.
Ten little Christmas reindeer.

FIVE LITTLE ELVES

This little elf went to the workshop
    (raise thumb, point it up)
This little elf stayed home
    (take index finger, point it up)
This little elf ate a candy cane
    (point to middle finger)
This little elf ate none
    (point to ring finger)
But this little elf cried, HO, HO, HO!
    (point to little finger)
Merry Christmas all the way home

SANTA'S COMING

Santa's on the roof top.
    (cup hand to ear)
Santa's in his sled.
He's coming down the chimney,
    (put thumb down)
I'd better jump in bed.
He's filled all the stockings,
    (raise hands to fill stockings)
And checking out the tree.
He's putting out the presents,
For all the family.

WAYS OF SAYING "HAPPY CHRISTMAS"

God Jul - Swedish and Norwegian
Feliz Natal - Portuguese
Frohliche Weihnachten - German
Buone Feste Natalizie - Italian

Joyeux Noel - French
Feliz Navidad - Spanish
Bozego Narodzenia - Polish
Galaedelig Jul - Danish

From Rhymes for Learning Times, by Louise Binder Scott
Copyright © T.S. Denison & Co., Inc.

CHRISTMAS LANGUAGE ACTIVITIES

A HOLIDAY WISH

The celebrations that occur during the month of December are all filled with gifts for children. It is nice to remind children that giving gifts to others is just as nice as receiving gifts. *(Although very young children may not believe you!)* Ask each of the children to tell you about a gift that their parents might like to receive. Tell the children something that you would like. Encourage them to think about others. Ask each of the children to make a special holiday wish. This wish should be for someone other than themselves. (Example: I hope baby brother gets a new rattle. I hope that Grandma gets a new purse, etc.)

Older children may enjoy using this topic as a creative writing assignment.

SANTA PUPPET

Many young children are fearful of visiting Santa in person. It is wonderful to hear how he is going to come down our chimney and leave presents, but ... when it is actually time to go and sit on his lap and verbally have to tell him what you want, well ... that is sometimes an entirely different story.

Provide the children with the experience of telling Santa what they would like by using a Santa Puppet. This will probably help make the experience of talking to the "real" Santa much easier.

LITTLE ELVES

Turn the following rhyme into a flannel board activity or use real objects. This rhyme will help children learn to identify and name colors as well as to rote count.

> One, two, three, four, five little elves.
> Putting toys on Santa's shelves.
> First little elf had something blue.
> 'Twas a small ballerina shoe.
> The second little elf had something red.
> It was a little girl's doll bed.
> Third little elf had something white.
> It was a truck shiny and bright.
> Fourth little elf had something brown.
> It was a funny talking clown.
> Fifth little elf had something black.
> It was his very own knapsack.

CHRISTMAS LANGUAGE ACTIVITIES

PRESENTS

Have six different presents drawn on the chalkboard with colored chalk. For skill in following directions and for the development of size concepts, ask the children to put an "X" over the biggest present or a circle around the pink present. Vary the direction and the concepts.

For older children you can use the colored chalk presents for practice in ordinal numbers. Circle the fifth present or circle the first present, etc.

SOUNDS WE HEAR

What sounds do we hear at Christmas? (Bells carols, people laughing, Ho, Ho ...). Ask the children to think up as many sounds as they can that remind them of the Christmas season. Make a tape recording of those sounds. Play the recording for the children. Have the children identify the sounds as they hear them. Make a picture chart of all the Christmas sounds.

DICTATE A LETTER

During the Hanukkah and Christmas seasons, many families are receiving various cards and letters of good wishes for a happy holiday season. Children not only enjoy receiving mail but even a very young child enjoys sending mail to someone special. Find the time and let each child in your class dictate a holiday letter to send to someone special. I would suspect that most young children would want to send a letter to their parents. This is a wonderful expressive language experience for a young child.

The teacher should add a "P.S." at the end of the letter for the child. Ask the child's special person to send a letter back to the child. Ask that the letter be sent to the school's address. The teacher should save the letters until every child in the class has received a response. Once all the letters have arrived, pass them out and during a group activity read each of the letters. *(Children really love this experience!)*

Older children may be able to write their own letters and read their own responses.

Help Rudolph Find The North Pole!

The
North Pole

Start

Name _____

COOKIE TREE

Give each of the children a large circle cut from a 9" x 11" piece of construction paper. This circle is a large cookie. Glue yarn around the edge of the cookie. Have the children cut out a winter or Christmas picture from old magazines to glue in the center of the circle. The children may also wish to draw their own pictures for the circle. Arrange the cookies on the bulletin board in the shape of a tree. Add a trunk.

CHRISTMAS BULLETIN BOARD

CLASSROOM TREE

 Cover the background of the bulletin board with a light color; blue, yellow, etc. Mount a large cut-out of a green tree. The tree should be big, wide, and cover as much of the bulletin board as possible. Let the children spend several days decorating the bulletin board tree. Locate a collection of used Christmas cards. Have the children cut pictures out of the discarded cards. Mount the pictures on colored construction paper and hang as ornaments on the bulletin board tree.

 Let the children be creative and design ornaments of their own. Provide the children with a variety of materials: buttons, glitter, sequins, material scraps, foil, etc. Paper chains are also a nice touch to give your classroom tree a finished look.

T'was The Night Before Christmas

*Write one sentence from the story **"T'was The Night Before Christmas."***
Draw a picture to go with the sentence.

_____

_ _

_____

_ _

_____

_ _

_____

Name _____

CHRISTMAS MUSIC ACTIVITIES

CHRISTMAS IS COMING

Christ - mas is com - ing, The goose is get - ting fat!

Please to put a pen - ny in an old man's hat, If you

hav - n't got a pen - ny a ha' - pen - ny will do, If you

hav - n't got a ha' - pen - ny, God bless you.

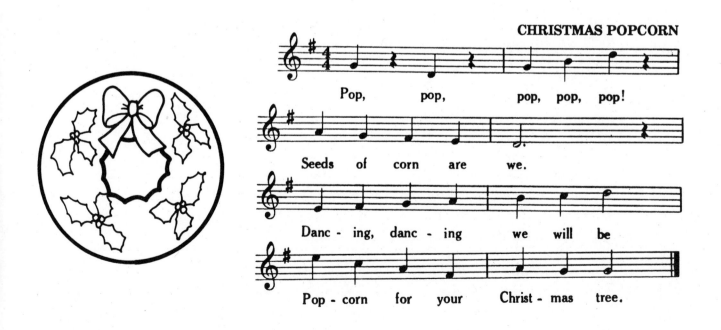

CHRISTMAS POPCORN

Pop, pop, pop, pop, pop!

Seeds of corn are we.

Danc - ing, danc - ing we will be

Pop - corn for your Christ - mas tree.

SUGGESTED READING LIST

dePaola, Tomie. ***Merry Christmas, Strega Nona***. Harcourt, Brace, Jovanovich. Copyright 1986. *Summary:* Big Anthony plans a surprise Christmas party for Strega Nona.

Devlin, Wende. ***Cranberry Christmas.*** Parents Magazine Press. Copyright © 1976. *Summary:* Mr. Whiskers faces a gloomy Christmas until Maggie and her Grandmother help him straighten out his house.

Dovoisin, Roger. ***The Christmas Whale.*** Knopf. Copyright © 1945. *Summary:* When Santa's reindeer get the flu a week before Christmas, the Whale comes to the rescue.

Gammel, Steven. ***Wake Up Bear...It's Christmas.*** Lothrop Lee and Shepard Books. Copyright © 1981. *Summary:* A hibernating bear wakes up on Christmas and entertains a special visitor.

Henry, Marie H. ***Bunnies At Christmas.*** Dial Books for Young Readers. Copyright © 1986. *Summary:* An invitation to Santa Claus to join the bunnies for a Christmas party, butUncle Jack comes instead, but he comes with toys and Santa whiskers.

Hutchins, Pat. ***The Silver Christmas Tree.*** MacMillan. Copyright © 1974. *Summary:* Squirrel wonders what happened to the beautiful star that had appeared at the top of his Christmas tree.

Keats, Ezra Jack. ***The Little Drummer Boy.*** MacMillan. Copyright © 1988. *Summary:* An illustrated version of the Christmas carol about the procession to Bethlehem and the offer of a poor boy to play his drum for the Christ child.

Low, Joseph. ***The Christmas Grump.*** Atheneum. Copyright © 1977. *Summary:* A mouse resents the fact that no presents are ever placed under the tree for him.

Parish, Peggy. ***Merry Christmas, Amelia Bedelia.*** Grennwillow Books. Copyright © 1986. *Summary:* As Amelia Bedelia helps Mrs. Rogers prepare for Christmas she creates lots of confusion.

Suess, Dr. ***How The Grinch Stole Christmas.*** Random. Copyright © 1957. *Summary:* The Grinch tries to stop Christmas from coming by stealing all the presents and food from the village. Much to his surprise Christmas comes anyway.

HANUKKAH

CONTENTS

CHANNUKAH (HANUKKAH)

Some children are not familiar with the miracle of the lamp in the temple; the meaning of the celebration of Hanukkah. Here is the story in a version that young children will understand.

HANUKKAH

This is the Jewish Holiday known as the Feast of Lights. This happy eight-day celebration comes in the winter and is a time of presents and parties.

Long ago, when a foreign king and his army took over Palestine and the temple there, the Jewish people fought their enemy for three years and at last they won. Lights were kept burning inside the temple, but finally there was only enough oil left for one more day. Then the great miracle occurred. The light burned for eight days and nights, giving the Jewish people enough time to prepare more oil.

Ever since then, Jewish people around the world celebrate Chanukah by lighting one candle each night of the eight nights until all are lit on the last day of the holiday. The menorah is a special nine-branched candelabra and is used for this holiday. One candle is used each night and the ninth branch holds an extra candle from which the other candles are lighted.

Bring a menorah into your classroom. Let the children see it, and have the opportunity of lighting the candles.

MENORAH

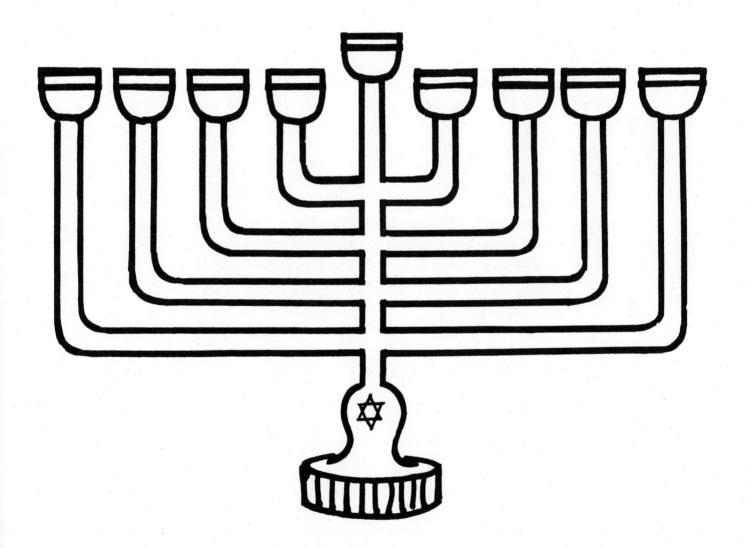

Use as a pattern or you may reproduce a menorah for each child in your class. The children may add construction paper candles.

HANUKKAH ART ACTIVITIES

WRAPPING PAPER

You will need: newsprint, tempera paint *(Hanukkah colors, blue and gold)* and paint brushes.

Pass out the newsprint to each child. Instruct them in how to fold the newsprint in half and then open. Have the children dip their brushes into the paint and have them drip the paint onto half of the paper. They should fold the paper closed again and rub the paper together with their hands. The paper is then opened and let to dry. Wrap presents for the parents in this unique paper.

WOODWORKING PROJECT

You will need: Holiday wrapping paper *(either Christmas or Hanukkah),* balsa wood, glue, an X-acto knife or razor blade, ribbon, paint brushes and felt.

What you do: The teacher should cut the balsa wood into squares for the children. Balsa wood is very easy to cut. The children can cut out a picture or a design from wrapping paper or the children may create their own Hanukkah drawing. Glue the picture onto the balsa wood. Glue ribbon around the picture, and glue a loop of ribbon on the back for a hanger. Glue a square of felt on the back of the balsa wood to give a nice finished look. The children now have a lovely Hanukkah wall hanging.

SPRAY LID WITH GOLD PAINT

JEWELRY CHEST

This is an easy-to-make gift, that looks most impressive when it is completed. The jewelry chest will make a nice Hanukkah gift for parents. You will need a cigar box for each child. (tobacco stores are usually very nice about donating as many as you will need), black enamel paint, gold spray paint, glue and black felt.

Paint the cigar box with black enemal. When it is dry, glue on different shapes of macaroni and noodles. Turn the box upside down with the lid open so it extends outward. Cover the box part with an old newspaper and spray the lid with gold paint. The inside of the box may be painted. Cut a piece of black felt the size of the bottom of the box. Glue this in the bottom of your jewelry chest. If desired, the entire chest may be lined with felt.

This is the season for giving gifts. What would you put in this present, and who would you give it to?

TO:

FROM:

HANUKKAH FINGER PLAYS/POETRY

THE DREIDEL

Nun, gimmel, hay, shin.
Put the nuts and candies in.
Take a dreidel from the shelf,
And let it spin and spin.
Nun means nothing if it shows.
Gimmel is one, a number small.
Hay means half of everything.
But shin means win and take it all.
Nun, gimmel, hay, shin.
Spin the dreidel on the floor.
Spin it like a spinning top,
One and two and three and four.

(A dreidel can be made from a square of styrofoam or a section of an egg carton. Number the sides and let numerals stand for the Hebrew letters. Add a zero for nun. Sharpen the end of a stick in the pencil sharpener and push it through the styrofoam to make a dreidel. Peanuts, raisins, or candy are divided equally among players. Everyone agrees on the number to be placed in a pile or dish. A child spins the dreidel or top, and if nun lands face up, the player gets nothing. No candy is put in the dish. If gimmel comes up, the player puts one candy into the dish. If hay lands face up, the player takes half of the candies. If shin shows, the player takes all the candies.)

*From Rhymes for Learning Times, by Louise Binder Scott
Copyright © T.S. Denison & Co., Inc.*

HANUKKAH IS HERE

One bright candle burning,
Through the winter night.
Hanukkah is here,
Hanukkah is here.
Two bright candles buring,
A festival of light.
Hanukkah is here,
Hanukkah is here.
(Continue until all eight candles are lighted. A mobile made of a wire coat hanger can be hung up; then stars of David covered with gold paper can be attached by string to the coat hanger.)
*From Rhymes for Learning Times
by Louise Binder Scott.
Copyright © T.S. Denison & Co., Inc.*

HANUKKAH LIGHTS

One light, two lights, three lights, and four.
     (hold up four fingers, one at a time)
Five lights, six lights, and three more;
     (hold up five more fingers)
Twinkle, twinkle, nine pretty lights
     (move fingers)
In a golden menorah bright!
     (cup palms of hands)
(Turn this into a flannel board activity by preparing a golden Menorah and nine candles.)
From Rhymes for Fingers and Flannel Boards, by Louise Binder Scott and J.J. Thompson. Copyright © T.S. Denison & Co., Inc.

HANUKKAH MUSIC ACTIVITIES

CANDLES OF HANUKKAH

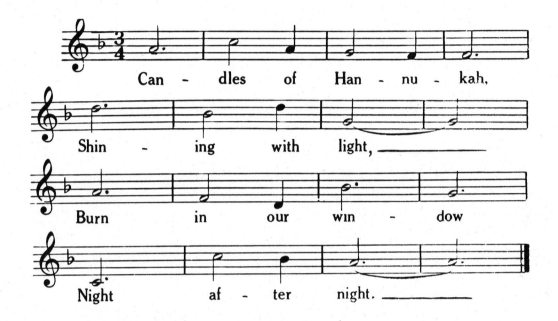

HANUKKAH IS COMING

SUGGESTED READING LIST

Abrason, Lillian S. ***Hannukkah Alphabet.*** Shulsinger Brothers. Copyright © 1968. *Summary:* Each letter of the alphabet introduces a word or name describing the customs and origins of Hanukkah.

Gellman, Ellie. ***Its Chanukah.*** Kar-Ben Copies. Copyright © 1985. *Summary:* During Hanukkah Gila counts candles, chocolate coins, and apples and finds things with different shapes and colors.

Goffstein, M.B. ***Laughing Latkes.*** Farrar, Straus, Giroux. Copyright © 1980. *Summary:* Speculates on a variety of reasons why latkes seem to be laughing at Hanukkah.

Green, Jacqueline Dembar. ***Nathan's Hanukkah Bargain.*** Kar-Ben Copies. Copyright © 1982. *Summary:* Nathan's unsuccessful search for a Hanukkah menorah takes a new turn when his Grandpa teaches him about old-fashioned bargaining.

Hirsh, Marilyn. ***I Love Hanukkah.*** Holiday House. Copyright © 1984. *Summary:* A boy describes his family's celebration of Hanukkah and all the things he likes about the holiday.

Zallien, Jane Breskin. ***Beni's First Chanukah.*** A. Holt. Copyright © 1988. *Summary:* On the first night of Hanukkah a young bear helps his mother prepare latkes, plays spin the dreidel and recites a prayer with his father.

SNOW PEOPLE

CONTENTS

SNOW PEOPLE ART ACTIVITIES

MARSHMALLOW SNOWMAN

Have the children attach three marshmallows together by using toothpicks. When the three marshmallows are together the children can glue on facial features and add yarn or fabric for a scarf. *(Please be sure that the children know that they are not to eat their marshmallow snowman. Emphasize that glue was used to finish the snowman, and that glue doesn't taste very good!)* These snowmen can be add to the table display described in the last activity on this page, *STAND-UP SNOW PEOPLE.*

VARIATION: You can make marshmallow snowpeople that can be eaten. Push the marshmallows onto a popsicle stick. Dip toothpicks in food coloring to add the facial features.

SAND PAINTING

You will need: 12" x 18" blue construction paper, white tempera paint, sand, Q-tips, large brushes and pie tins.

Draw two circles on blue paper for the snow person's body. Mix two tablespooons of sand to each cup of paint. Place the paint and sand in pie tins. Pass out the blue paper and large brushes. Have the children paint the inside of the circles. Paint snowflakes with the Q-tips. When the paint is dry, the children can add facial features with markers.

STAND-UP SNOWPEOPLE

Most all classrooms make snow people during the winter months and display them on a wall or bulletin board. Stand-up snow people are a little different and make a wonderful table display. Have each of the children cut out the shape of a snow person *(The teacher may wish to pre-cut these shapes for younger children)*. Have the children cover the snow person with cotton and use glitter, buttons, and scrap fabric for the acessories.

When the snow people are completed tape a brace on the back of each snow person so it may stand up. Cover a table with cotton batting, pinecones, small twigs and braches to represent trees, and display the snow people among the winter scene. This makes a very attractive display and one that the children can actually have fun playing with and rearranging.

FINISH THE SNOW PEOPLE!

Look at all the shapes of the snow people. No one ever finished building the snow people! Finish the snow people by drawing facial features and adding hats, scarfs, or anything that you would like the snow people to have. Try to make each of the snow people look different.

Name _____

THE SNOWMAN

The children can pretend to be the snowman, or some can pretend to be the children working on the snowman.

The snowman **stood tall and very straight** for many days after the new snow. Then the sun shone brightly and the warm winds blew. The snowman began **frowning** and was sad, for he knew that he was melting. Slowly his shoulders began to **droop,** and he **bent forward** and then **backward from his middle, to one side and then the other.** He felt his head as it began to **slide** off his chest. It was turning **around and around.** He **leaned forward** and then **backwar**d to keep it from sliding farther. The snowman **caught his head** in his stick hands just in time. He could feel himself shrink, **getting smaller and smaller, bending his legs, squatting** - his bottom half was disappearing into the ground. Suddenly he **fell over** on the ground and his body fell apart. He couldn't move. The poor snowman was so unhappy and he began to **cry.**

The sun set and darkness covered the sky with heavy gray fluffy clouds. The winds changed, sweeping cold chilling air across the snowman. His tears turned to icicles and he **smiled** again. It was snowing!

The next morning the children **dashed** outside to have a snowball fight and to repair the snowman. The children **rolled a big ball, packing it hard, then a second snowball.** The snowman was growing again. The children **placed** the heavy balls on top of each other. There he was - bottom and chest but no head! The children delicately **replaced** the eyes. They **gave** him a carrot nose which **wiggled** and a big **smile** made of wood so it would last all year. Two rocks were added for floppy ears, and he had a huge cowboy hat. The children carefully **placed** the head on the rest of the body and once again the snowman **stood straight and tall.** He was very happy.

From Fun with Action Stories, by Joan Daniels.
Copyright © T.S. Denison & Co., Inc.

'SNOWFLAKE' THE SNOW PERSON

Color the pieces of the snowperson.
Cut them out. Paste them on a piece
of paper. Now you have made "Snowflake",
the Snowperson.

FIVE LITTLE SNOW PEOPLE

Five little snow people, five little
    snow people,
Sat upon the ground.
> *(Teacher holds up five fingers;
> five children stand in a row)*

Every little snow person, every little
    snow person,
Was so fat and round.

The first little snow person, first little
    snow person,
Said, "I want to stay."
The sun began a-shining, sun began a-
    shining,
So she went away.
> *(first child sinks to the floor)*

The second little snow person, second
    little snow person,
Looked so neat and trim.
He was very sleepy, he was very sleepy,
That was all of him.
> *(second child sinks to the floor)*

The third little snow person, third little
    snow person,
Saw a sled go by.
So she went a-sledding, so she went a-
    sledding,
And she said, "Good-bye."
> *(third child sinks to the floor)*

The fourth little snow person, fourth
    little snow person,
Stood straight and tall.
His feet were slowly melting, his feet
    were slowly melting,
And he took a fall. Oh ...!
> *(fourth child sinks to the floor)*

The fifth little snow person, fifth little
    snow person,
Said, "I want a song,
Sing it very quickly, sing it very quickly,
I can't stay too long!"
> *(fifth child sinks to the floor)*

Five little snow people, five little snow
    people,
Made of ice and snow.
We would like to keep you, we would like
    to keep you,
Please, oh, please, don't go!
> *(repeat with five other children)*

Use as a flannel board story. The patterns are found on pages 71 & 72.

PATTERNS

Patterns for the story, "Five Little Snow People,"
found on page 70.

PATTERNS

Patterns for the story, "Five Little Snow People,"
found on page 70.

SNOW PEOPLE LEARNING GAMES

TALL AND SHORT SNOWPEOPLE
The teacher will need to pre-cut many white felt circles. A few of the circles should have faces. Make a snow person on the flannel board for the children to look at. Show the children how you put the circles on top of each other to make a snow person. Now make a tall snow person and a short snow person. Talk about the differences in the snow people. Let the children make tall and short snow people.

These circles can also be used for addition and subtraction facts. If we have a snow person made of four snowballs and we take away one of the snowballs how big is the snowperson now?

SNOW PEOPLE COOKIES
Decorating cookies is tons of fun for young children. Here is an easy and extremely successful idea.

Purchase some rolls of sugar cookie dough. Bake the cookies according to the directions on the package. Let each child frost a cookies with white frosting. Sprinkle shredded coconut on the frosting. Raisins can be added for facial features. Each child has now made their own "snow person cookie." Not only are these cookies fun to make, but they are great to eat!

PIN THE HAT ON THE SNOWMAN
This game is played just like *"Pin The Tail On The Donkey."* The teacher should make a large snowman that can be hung on the wall. Each child should have a black construction paper hat. Blindfold the children *(for children fearful of blindfold, use an old pair of sunglasses with the lenses painted black.)* Each child should have a turn to try and pin the hat to the top of the snowman's head.

Snow People Practice

Name_____

Teachers, design your own activity page for the children.

SUGGESTED READING LIST

Briggs, Raymond. *The Snowman.* Random House. Copyright © 1978.
   Summary: When a snowman comes to life, a little boy invites him home
   and in return is taken on a flight above beautiful cities and strange lands.

Goffstein, M.B. *Our Snowman*. Harper & Row. Copyright © 1986.
   Summary: The snowman two children build looks so lonely when night
   comes that the little girl and her father go out to make him a wife.

Lobe, Mira. *The Snowman Who Went For A Walk.* W. Morrow. Copyright
   © 1984. *Summary:* A snowman becomes able to walk and decides to find
   a place where he can never melt.

The Snowman. (Video Cassette) Weston Books. Copyright © 1983. Copies
   distributed by Sony. *Summary:* An animated film in which a young boy
   dreams that his snowman comes to life and they share the adventures of
   Christmas and winter.

Wegen, Ron. *Sky Dragon.* Greenwillow Books. Copyright © 1982. *Summary:*
   The children look up at the snow-filled clouds in the sky and see them as
   various animals which gives them an idea on what to build with the snow.

MARTIN LUTHER KING DAY

CONTENTS

WHO WAS MARTIN LUTHER KING, JR.?

In 1983, Congress established the third Monday in January, beginning in 1986, as a federal holiday in honor of the birth of Martin Luther King. This honor was created so we could all honor a great American black leader who practiced peaceful demonstration for equal rights.

Martin Luther King was born in Atlanta, Georgia in January 15, 1929, the son of Baptist Ministers. He graduated from Morehouse College at the age of 19. Three years later he earned the bachelor of divinity degree at Crozer Theological Seminary and in 1955 he was awarded a Ph.D. at Boston University.

Martin Luther King believed in equality for all people and worked very hard against prejudice and discrimination. Through all his work fighting prejudice Dr. King believed in peaceful solutions. He was quoted as saying, "We will not resort to violence. We will not degrade ourselves with hatred. Love will be returned for hate."

In December 1955, Martin Luther King began a campaign in Montgomery, Alabama against laws that required segregation on buses. *(Explain to the children what bus segregation was.)* After a year of very difficult times, blacks and whites rode Montgomery buses on an unsegregated basis for the first time. The United States Supreme Court had ruled the Alabama segregation bus laws as unconstitutional. The challenges in Montgomery, Alabama had taught the black Americans the power of organization and the dignity of nonviolence.

Dr. King achieved his goals through demonstrations, marches, speeches, and peaceful actions. Probably his most famous demonstration was the *"March on Washington."* On August 28, 1963, 250,000 Americans of all faiths, races, and creeds joined him in a demonstration in solidarity. It was at this march in Washington where Dr. King delivered one of his most impressive speeches. "I have a dream" he said. A dream of the time when the evils of prejudice and segregation will vanish.

In 1964, Martin Luther King was awarded the Nobel Peace prize for his work in civil rights.

Unfortunately, Martin Luther King was shot and killed on April 4, 1968 in Memphis, Tennessee, and our whole country lost a great leader.

Martin Luther King

(1929 - 1968)

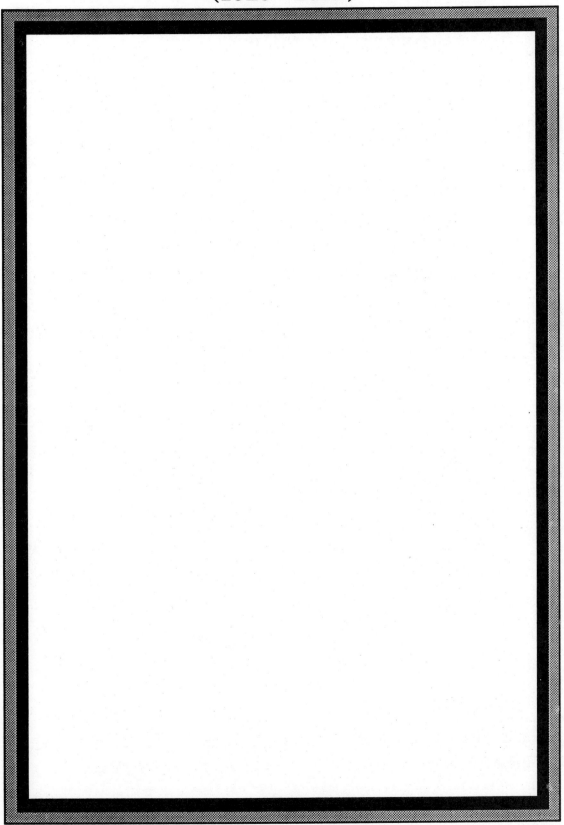

Draw a picture of this famous American Leader.   Name _____

MARTIN LUTHER KING ACTIVITIES

MARTIN LUTHER KING, JR.

Martin Luther King's birthday is a national holiday. Young children may not understand the importance of Dr. King's work and the significant effect he had in our country; but children are not too young to learn his name and some of the highlights of his life. Read "Who Was Martin Luther King" *(page 78)* to the children. Discuss unfamiliar vocabulary words. Coorelate equal rights to sharing and taking turns. Explain how discussion and cooperation means peaceful problem solving. Peaceful problem solving is more effective than fighting.

PEOPLE ARE IMPORTANT

Take pictures of the children in your class as they are playing and participating in some of the routine activities in your calssroom. Take pictures of them sharing, taking turns, and working cooperatively. Capture moments of harmony. Point out how well the children are working together and what good friends they are. The children will enjoy discussing the pictures and finding pictures of themselves.

HAPPY BIRTHDAY MARTIN LUTHER KING

After talking about Martin Luther King and learning why we celebrate his birthday, talk about friendship.

Then have the children trace the shape of one of their hands on a piece of construction paper. Cut out the hands. Tape all the hands on a wall in your classroom, overlapping them so it looks like they are holding hands. Create a caption to put over the hands.

MARTIN LUTHER KING - A POEM

A man named Martin Luther King
Gave us a new song to sing.
A black man, a minister's son,
Told us we could overcome.
Equality will be our right,
And brotherhood will shine its light.

Martin Luther King stepped out;
Told us how, without a doubt.
Equality would march on through,
With brotherhood for me and you.
*(Show the children photographs
of Martin Luther King.)*

Martin Luther King tried to solve problems peacefully. Write about a problem that you have had. How did you solve your problem?

Name _____

HAVE YOU MADE SOMEONE HAPPY TODAY?

The teacher and the children should discuss what kinds of actions will make others happy in the classroom: sharing, taking turns, displaying affection, kindness, etc. Find pictures in magazines of the behaviors that the children mentioned. Display the pictures on the bulletin board. Let each child place a card with their name on it, or a picture of themself next to the picture that displays the behavior that makes the child happy. This is a good bulletin board for encouraging positive interpersonal relationships and for encouraging expressive language skills.

Martin Luther King Day

He had a dream and worked for equal rights

Color the picture. Tell the children that Dr. King's most famous speech talked about his dream of equality and brotherhood for all people in the future.

SUGGESTED READING LIST

dePaola, Tomie. ***Oliver Button Is A Sissy.*** Harcourt. Copyright © 1979.
Summary: Oliver Button was called a sissy. He didn't like to do the things
that boys are suppose to do. He joins a tapdancing class and practices
hard, despite the teasing from the older boys.

Hope, Christopher. ***The Dragon Wore Pink.*** Atheneum. Copyright © 1985.
Summary: A dragon and a little girl, both outcasts, become friends and
help bring people and dragons together at a time when they both need
each other.

Lionni, Leo. ***Little Blue and Little Yellow.*** Obolensky. Copyright © 1959.

Suess, Dr. ***The Sneetches and Other Stories.*** Random. Copyright © 1961.
Summary: A variety of stories. The plain-bellied Sneetches and the star-
bellied Sneetches can't decide who is the better Sneetch. After many trips
through the star-on and the star-off machine no one can tell the difference
between the Sneetches.

Waber, Bernard. ***Lovable Lyle.*** Houghton. Copyright © 1969. *Summary:*
Lyle, the Crocodile thought everyone loved him until the day he received
a hate note from an anonymous despiser.

ANIMALS OF THE ARCTIC NORTH

─── CONTENTS ───

ANIMALS OF THE ARCTIC NORTH

The following is some information about some of the types of animals that live in the Arctic North. Go to the public library and locate some picture books that you can show the children. The animals of the north are fascinating and will probably be new for many of the children.

POLAR BEAR - Polar Bears live on the ice and cold water of the Arctic Ocean. Some live in Alaska, Canada, Greenland and Siberia. Polar Bears are white and grow to be 9 and one-half feet tall and can weigh up to 1,000 pounds. They keep warm with their thick coats of fur. The polar bear is a powerful swimmer. They like to catch seals, walrus and fish.

RIGHT WHALE - There are many different kinds of whales. The Right Whale lives in the cold North Atlantic Ocean. The Right Whale is very big, about 55 feet long and is usually black in color. A whale is not a fish. A whale is a mammal. A whale would drown if it stayed under the water all the time as fish do. A whale needs to breath air just like people. Whales do not lay eggs like fish. Whales give birth to their babies and nurse them with milk.

ARCTIC WOLF - The Arctic Wolf is sometimes called the White Wolf. They live in Artic North America and Greenland. They are very big wolves and weigh about 100 pounds. These Arctic Wolves are also called Tundra Wolves because they like to live in the tundra where there are no trees.

ARCTIC HARE - The Arctic Hare is a rabbit who has a beautiful white coat of fur.

HOODED SEAL/RINGED SEAL/RIBBON SEAL - Theses are some of the types of seals that live or travel to the Arctic Ocean. Seals have flippers which help them to be excellent swimmers. Seals are able to stay in the water for very long periods of time. They breath air like we do but they can stay under water for 10 to 30 minutes. *(We couldn't do that!)*

WOLVERINE - A Wolverine looks something like a bear but it cannot climb trees like bears do. It is a short animal about 2 and a half feet long. It has shaggy fur. The Wolverine is very fierce and is one of the most powerful animals for its size in the world. Wolverines live in Canada and North America and are relatives of badgers, skunks and otters.

WALRUS - Walruses live very near the North Pole. They like to live on drifting pack ice but will come ashore. The word *Walrus* comes from the Scandinavian word which means *Whale Horse*. The Walrus looks like a seal but has long tusks which come down from the upper jaw. A full-grown Walrus is about 10 feet long and may weigh up to 3,000 pounds. In water a Walrus can move very fast but on land the Walrus is slow and clumsy. Walruses live together in herds. They are not harmful but will come to the aid of another Walrus if they believe it is being attacked.

MUSK OX - The Musk Ox is a shaggy looking animal which looks like a cross between an ox and a sheep. They are called Musk Ox because of the musk-like odor they give off when excited. They are very big animals, usually from 7 to 8 feet long and 4 to 5 feet high. Sometimes their hair gets so long that it touches the ground.

If you were an animal that lived in the north, what type of animal would you like to be? Draw a picture of that animal.

Write the name of the animal.

Artic Animal Activities

WALRUS WALK

Show the children pictures of walruses. Do walruses have feet? Can walruses walk on the ground? Could a walrus run? Jump? Move quickly on the ground? How do you think a walrus moves on the ground? Have the children pretend to be a walrus and move about the room as a walrus would. When the children have mastered how they think a walrus would move, organize some walrus running races.

POLAR BEAR

Provide each of the children with a heavy sheet of paper with an outline of a polar bear on it. Older children may wish to draw their own polar bear. Next, mix flaked soap with water to make a thick mixture. The children can paint their polar bears with this mixture to give the polar bears an interesting texture. Add bits of paper or seeds for the bear's facial features.

WALRUS

Show the children a large picture or drawing of a walrus. Have the children draw a picture of a walrus. Discuss with the children the shape of the walrus, the tusks and the flippers. After the children have completed their drawings, the children may color or paint their walrus and glue on toothpicks for the tusks.

ARCTIC ANIMALS

Which animals do not belong in the picture?

Name _____

ARTIC ANIMAL BULLETIN BOARD

ANIMALS OF THE ARCTIC NORTH

The teacher should cover a bulletin board in white paper or tape a large sheet of white paper to the wall. Let the children have fun painting a mural scene of the northern arctic region. After the scenery is completed, using the information gained from *Animals of the Arctic North on page 86,* have the children create pictures of the northern animals and add these to the mural.

ARCTIC ANIMALS

Name _____

CROSSWORD PUZZLE

WORD BANK

Wolf
Seal
Whale
Snow
Bear
Walrus

ACROSS

2. An excellent swimmer with flippers who can stay under water for up to 30 minutes.

3. A large animal with tusks, who swims well but is clumsy on land.

5. An dog-like animal covered with fur that is sometimes white.

DOWN

1. A large animal that is covered with thick white fur. It is a Polar _____.

3. This large animal looks like a fish but is really a mammal that always stays in the water.

4. Arctic animals love to play in the _____.

ARCTIC ANIMAL MUSIC

COLD SWIMMING FUN
(Sung to the tune of "London Bridges")

Polar Bears have swimming fun.
Swimming fun, swimming fun.
Polar Bears have swimming fun.
They love cold water.
(Other verses can be sung by changing "Polar Bear" to "Seals, Whales, and Walruses.")

ANIMALS WHO LIKE THE COLD
(Sung to the tune of "Twinkle, Twinkle Little Star")

How many animals like the cold.
Many animals it is told.

Polar Bear and the Walrus,
Pretty White Wolves and Musk Ox.

How many animals like the cold.
Many animals it is told.

ARCTIC ANIMAL PATTERNS

Here are some patterns of animals that enjoy either the snow or playing in cold water.
Turn them into flannel board patterns or stick puppets and let the children
make up their own stories about these animals

ARCTIC ANIMAL PATTERNS

Here are some patterns of animals that enjoy either the snow or playing in cold water.
Turn them into flannel board patterns or stick puppets and let the children
make up their own stories about these animals

SUGGESTED READING LIST

Hall, Derek. **Polar Bear Leaps.** Sierra Club - Knopf. Distributed by Random House. Copyright © 1985. *Summary:* Baby Polar Bear goes fishing with his mother and learns that a leap to safety can save his life.

Hoff, Syd. **Walpole.** Harper. Copyright © 1977. *Summary:* Although Walpole is the biggest walrus in the herd he would rather play with the baby walruses than to be a leader.

Stevenson, James. **Winston, Newton, Elton and Ed.** Greenwillow Books. Copyright © 1978. *Summary:* Two stories featuring 3 pugnacious walruses, the second, a stranded penguin.

Stone, Lynn. **The Arctic.** Children's Press. Copyright © 1985. *Summary:* Describes the arctic, including its seasons, geographical features, animal life and people.

Yulla. **Polar Bear Brothers.** Harper. Copyright © 1960. *Summary:* A young Polar Bear and his brother spend time playing in their pool.

GROUNDHOG DAY

CONTENTS

SHADOW LEARNING GAMES

SHADOWS AND MR. GROUNDHOG

• Be sure to explain to the children what a groundhog is and what is suppose to happen when he sees or does not see his shadow. Show the children pictures of real groundhogs that you have found in books.

• Groundhog Day is a wonderful time to provide your children with shadow activities. Take the children outside and see if they can see their own shadows.

• Hang a sheet by stretching a rope between two points; for example, in a doorway or in a corner of the room. Place a light source *(spot light, overhead projector, lamp without a shade, flashlight, etc.)* behind the sheet, facing it so that it's shining toward the sheet.

Divide the class in half - one group will be the audience, the other group will be the performers. Have each performer choose an object from the list of objects below. Turn the light source off, position the child in a profile position behind the sheet, and have the child hold up the chosen object. Turn the light source on.

The audience must guess what object is being held up and who is holding it up. After each of the children in the first group has had a turn, switch groups. Be sure to turn the light source off between each child, so that his/her identity will be a secret until it's time for the audience to guess.

Shadow Objects:

chair	numeral and letter cut-outs	coat
ball	opened book	pants
jump rope	doll	hand
pencil	housekeeping items	purse
shoe	truck	piece of paper
puzzle piece	block	large paper clip

• Have the children choose partners and trace each other's shadows.

• Put a filmstrip projector in your room and have the children experiment with hand shadows.

• Look for shadows in the classroom.

STANDING GROUNDHOG

Color and cut out the groundhog. Tape a cardboard brace on the back of the groundhog so he may stand-up. Take the standing groundhog outside and check for his shadow.

Did The Groundhog See His Shadow?

Color the groundhog. Add a shadow if the groundhog saw his shadow today. Do NOT
draw a shadow if the groundhog did NOT see his shadow today.
Write a sentence about your picture.

_____

_____

_____

_____

Name _____

GROUNDHOG DAY RHYMES

FEBRUARY SECOND
(Two may perform this action play. One is groundhog. One is Shadow.)

Down in his burrow, deep in the ground,
  (Groundhog curled up asleep)
Groundhog wakes and begins to stir
around.
  (wakes, stretches, yawns)
"I've slept enough! On this February
day, I think it would be nice to go up and
play!"

Up - up - up! He pokes his head out,
  (gets up slowly)
Looks this way and that way - looks all
about.
  (looks all around)
Then, out jumps Groundhog.
The day is clear and bright.
  (jumps)
He sits beside his hole in the warm
sunlight.
  (sits down)

Sneaking up behind him - Groundhog
does not see ...
  (shadow creeps up behind groundhog)
Shadow comes a'creeping, quiet as can
be.
Groundhog looks around.
He trembles with great fear.
  *(Groundhog looks over shoulder and
  trembles)*

"Boo!" shouts Shadow. "Get out of here!"
"Shoo! Shoo, Groundhog! You cannot
stay!"
  *(Shadow makes shooing and waving
  motions)*
Down scurries groundhog until another
day!
  *(Groundhog dives down - curls up in
  a ball)*

THE SECOND OF FEBRUARY
There's only one day the whole year long
That I hope and pray the sun won't appear.
The Second of February, you all know,
The groundhog goes searching for his shadow.
If he should find it, the story is told,
We'll have six more weeks of winter's cold.
But if it is cloudy, his shadow's not there,
There'll soon be warm weather and days will be fair.
So please Mr. Sun, for just this one day,
Find a big, dark cloud - AND STAY AWAY!

OUT POPS MR. GROUNDHOG!

Directions: Color the groundhog and cut him out. Tape the ground to a popsicle stick. Color the entrance to the groundhog's house. Cut an opening on the dotted line. Now you can make the groundhog go in and out of his house.

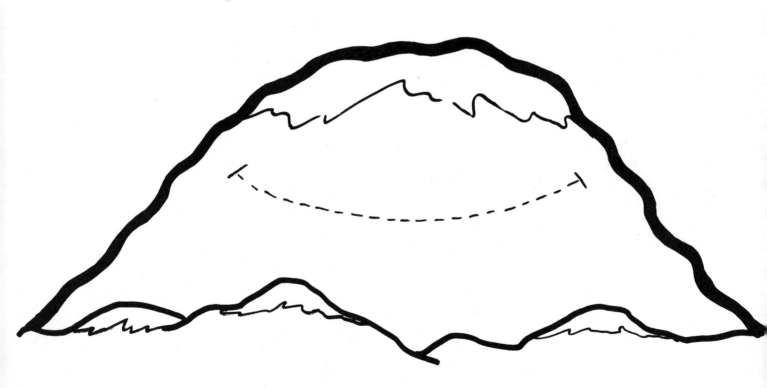

A Shadow Story

SHERRY'S SHADOW

Today I want to read you a poem about a little shadow. You have all seen your shadow when the sun comes out, haven't you, and your shadow tags right along with you - no matter where you go. This poem tells about a shadow that belongs to a little girl named Sherry.

(Display picture and shadow No. 1)
Sherry had a shadow
Who was bashful - Who was shy;
But Sherry always saw her
When the sun shown in the sky.
    (Remove Pictures)

(Display picture and shadow No. 2)
When Sherry ran along the walk,
That's what her friend would do -
    (Remove Pictures)
(Display picture and shadow No. 3)
If Sherry stood upon her head,
The shadow stood there too!
    (Remove pictures)

When Sherry turned a somer-
sault,
Her shadow helped her turn it;
(Display picture and shadow No. 4)
If Sherry wanted to jump rope,
The show-off also twirled it.
    (Remove pictures)

(Display picture and shadow No. 1)
"Shame on you, old shadow!"
Sherry said to her one day.
"You should not copy what I do,
Why don't you just go away?"

And then the yellow sunshine
Surely hid behind a tree,
For Sherry's little shadow
Vanished almost instantly!
    (Remove shadow)

"Please come on back, my
shadow!"
Sherry shouted to her friend,
"I shall not scold you anymore -
Dash back and play again!"

Just then the sun shone
brightly,
And as Sherry blinked her eyes,
    (Replace shadow)
Up popped the bashful shadow,
Blinking at the sunny skies!

"Hi there, show-off Shadow!
I'll race you down the street!"
    (Remove pictures)
(Display picture and shadow No.2)
Then Sherry and her shadow
Dashed off with flying feet!

*(Use as a flannel board story. The
patterns are found on pages 104 & 105)*

*From Learning To Lister, by Celestine Houston.
Copyright © T.S. Denison & Co., Inc.*

STORY PATTERNS

Patterns from the story, Sherry's Shadow, found on page 103.

No. 1

No. 2

STORY PATTERNS

Patterns from the story, Sherry's Shadow, found on page 103.

No. 3

No. 4

SUGGESTED READING LIST

Balian, Corna. ***A Garden for a Groundhog.*** Abingdon Press. Copyright ©
1985. *Summary:* Mr. O'Leary appreciates his groundhog's help in
predicting the weather on Groundhog Day but tries to come up with a
plan to keep him from eating all the vegetables in the garden.

Delton, Judy. ***Groundhog's Day At The Doctor.*** Parents Magazine Press.
Copyright © 1981. *Summary:* Groundhog visits the doctor and dispenses
his own medical advice while there.

Kesselman, Wendy. ***Time for Jody.*** Harper. Copyright © 1975. *Summary:*
Jody a groundhog loves to sleep. She is invited to wake the animals for
spring, but how can she wake herself up?

Kroll, Steven. ***It's Groundhog Day.*** Holiday House. Copyright © 1987.
Summary: Worried that an early spring will ruin his ski lodge business,
Roland Raccoon takes drastic steps to prevent Godfrey Groundhog from
looking for his shadow on Groundhog Day.

VALENTINE'S DAY

CONTENTS

Valentine's Day Art Activities

CROWNS

This art project is a lot of fun when it is used in conjunction with the rhyme, *"The Queen of Hearts,"* found on page 117.

To make the crown use shelf or finger painting paper, 4" x 24". Staple to fit the head size. Fold the band in half three times. Cut a point at the top. The crown may be decorated.

SPONGE HEART

The teacher should pre-cut sponges into the shape of hearts. Have the children dip the sponge hearts into red or pink paint and print the heart onto white paper. Children love sponge painting and with sponges pre-cut into the shapes the children will discover tremendous success.

VALENTINE MAIL BOXES

One of the best types of Valentine's Day mail boxes are made from old Kleenex tissue boxes. The small, tall boxes work the very best. On the first day have the children paint the boxes white or cover the boxes in white or pink construction paper. Provide the children with a multitude of materials for decorating their boxes: foil, tissue paper, sequins, buttons, colored paper, wrapping paper, greeting cards, doilies, glitter, etc.

Display on a table or window ledge. Label your display, "The Valentine's Day Post Office."

VALENTINE BIRD

Give each of the children three medium sized hearts, one circle and two tiny hearts. Show the children a finished Valentine Bird *(use the illustration next to this activity)* that you have previously put together. Ask the children if they can arrange their shapes into the bird, they may then glue the pieces onto construction paper.

Older children will want to cut out their own hearts and circle.

VALENTINE'S DAY ART ACTIVITIES

GLITTER HEARTS

Provide each of the children with a large sheet of construction paper. The construction paper should have the shape of a heart pre-drawn on the paper. *(Older children may draw their own heart.)* Let the children paint the inside of the heart with a color of their choice. When the paint is still wet, glitter may be sprinkled on the heart. (It is advisable to place the wet painting in a 9" x 13" cake pan. The glitter will stay in the cake pan and not create a large mess.)

When the paint and glitter is dry, the heart may be cut out. Hang the glitter hearts from the ceiling of the classroom.

VALENTINE CARDS FOR MOM AND DAD

Fold red construction paper in half. Cut out a white heart (or use a white doily) and paste on the front of the card. On the inside of the card print:

> *Someone loves you*
> *Do you know who?*
> *Take a look inside and see*
> *The one who loves you is me.*

On the inside of the card, paste a picture of the child. Use a school picture or a polaroid picture.

CRAYON CHIP HEART

You will need: White finger paint
Wax paper
Red crayon chips
Iron
Scissors

What you do: Pre-trace the shape of a heart on white paper. Pass out the paper and crayon chips. Have the children sprinkle the chips inside the heart. Place wax paper on top and iron it quickly and lightly. Have the children cut out the hearts through both layers and hang them on your windows.

Decorate the Heart

Name _____

VALENTINE'S DAY RECIPES

TARTS

Prepare a pie crust (using a frozen pie crust or one which comes in a box is easier). Using cookie cutters, cut two small circles for each tart. Cut a small circle from the center of one of the circles. Bake and put together with jam or jelly.

Children will enjoy using the cookie cutters and filling the tarts with the jam or jelly.

PUNCH

This is a very easy punch to make and the children will love it. Fill a large bowl with clear soda drink such as 7-Up or Sprite. Add some red fruit punch and top with raspberry or strawberry sherbet. This drink looks "fancy" and will add a festive touch to your Valentine party.

STRAWBERRY SHAKES

Strawberry shakes make a fun Valentine's Day party treat. Bring a blender into the classroom so the children can observe and assist with making the strawberry shakes.

Put vanilla ice cream, milk and fresh or frozen strawberries into the blender. Top each child's shake with a strawberry. Serve in paper cups for easy clean-up.

VALENTINE'S DAY WORDS

Look at each letter. Write a word on the line that begins with that letter.

V _____

A _____

L _____

E _____

N _____

T _____

I _____

N _____

E _____

S _____

D _____

A _____

Y _____

VALENTINE'S DAY LANGUAGE ACTIVITIES

MANY/FEW

You can use a number of objects with this activity, but for the sake of keeping with the Valentine holiday, use a variety of pre-cut hearts (or heart candy!)

Place a few hearts on one plate and many hearts on another plate. Discuss the plates with the children. Next ask the children to fill the plates. Vary whether you ask for just a few or for many. Older children can work on the concepts of greater than and less than with the heart candy.

WHAT IS A GOOD FRIEND?

Valentine's Day is a day when we often talk about love. With young children I think it is important to talk about "Friendship." What is a good friend? What things do friends do for one another? How can we try to be better friends? Do friends sometimes argue? Do friends take turns? Do friends share? Do friends try to remember to use good manners? What do you like to do with a good friend? Who are some of your good friends? *(Don't forget to mention that teachers are good friends too!)*

Older children may enjoy using these discussion topics as creative writing exercises.

THOUGHTFULNESS

Valentine's Day is a holiday when we remember to be thoughtful of one another and to say nice things to those people that we care about. Discuss Valentine's Day with your class. Ask the children to name some of the people in their lives that they would like to give a Valentine to. Ask the children who they think will give them a Valentine. Ask the children if they know what the word "thoughtfulness" means. What are some nice things that the children could do at home that their parents would appreciate? What are some things that the children could do at school that would be appreciated by the teachers.

HEART PUZZLE

Name_____

Cut, Paste, Color.

THE VALENTINE PARTY

The children can pretend they are the children in the class,
pantomiming the actions.

It was February 14th, Valentine's Day, and Tom's school class was ready for the Valentine Party. The helping parents were in charge and the children were seated at their desks. They first **passed out** their Valentine cards to everyone. With their bundles, they **walked around the room, placing** the cards on the desks.

It was soon time for a game. The first one was "Pin the Arrow on the Heart." The children were blindfolded *(close eyes)* and **spun around** several times. The class was so dizzy that they **almost fell over**. The children tried to find the big heart on the blackboard. They **walked forward**; no, wrong way. They **turned left, then to the right, taking four steps**. They **felt** the blackboard and **pinned** the arrows on it. The **blindfolds were removed** and **eyes opened**. The class had pinned the arrows on the school calendar.

The next game was a race. Everyone was given a suitcase filled with clothes which they had to put on in the proper order. Then they were to run to the other end of the room, take the clothes off, and replace them in the suitcase. Ready? **Open the suitcase, put on the baggy pants, rain hat, rain coat, boots, gloves and open the umbrella. Run** to the other side of the room. Now **close the umbrella, take off the gloves, boots, rain coat, rain hat and pants and put everything back in the suitcase. Sit down quietly.**

The next game was "Cupid Says," played like "Simon Says." Cupid says **do four jumping jacks**. Run in place. Cupid says **swing your arms in circles without touching anyone**. Cupid says **hop seven times on the right foot**. Hop on the left foot. Cupid says **hop ten times on both feet**. Skip around the room. Cupid says **stretch and reach for the ceiling, standing on tiptoes**. Bend down. Cupid says **walk around like a duck**. Cupid says **bend up and down to touch your toes ten times**. Stop! Cupid says **put hands on your waist, lean to the right, back, right and front five times**. Cupid says **sit down in your desk**. Who wins?

It was soon time for refreshments. The children enjoyed **eating** the chewy cupcakes and heart candies and **opening** their Valentine cards. It was a nice party.

From Fun with Action Stories, by Joan Daniels.
Copyright © T.S. Denison & Co., Inc.

COLOR THE HEARTS

Can you make each heart look different?

Name _____

Valentine's Day Rhymes/Poetry

FOR VALENTINE'S DAY
Flowers are sweet.
That is true.   *(nod head)*
But for my Valentine,   *(point at self)*
I'll choose you!   *(point at someone else)*
(And you and you and you!)   *(point at many at one time)*

THE QUEEN OF HEARTS
The Queen of Hearts,
She made some tarts,
All on a summer's day.
The Knave of Hearts,
He stole the tarts,
And took them clean away.
The King of Hearts,
Called for the tarts,
And told the Knave no more.
The Knave of Hearts,
Brought back the tarts,
And vowed he'd steal no more.

MY VALENTINE
My Valentine is red.
    (nod head)
My Valentine is blue.
    (point to self)
We'll cut and cut
    (make cutting motion)
And glue and glue
Then send it home to you
    (point to children one by one)
    and you and you.
(Have the children decorate the
Valentine on this page and send
it to someone of their choice.)

MY VALENTINE
My Valentine is red.
My Valentine is blue.
We'll cut and cut
And glue and glue
Then send it home to you
    and you and you.

LOOK-A-LIKE
VALENTINES

Directions: Draw a heart that looks just like the heart in each box.

VALENTINE'S DAY PARTY GAMES

DROPPING THE VALENTINE

Have the children sit in a circle. Give one child a Valentine. The child with the Valentine walks around the outside of the circle and puts the Valentine behind a child of their choice. The child who was given the Valentine gets up and chases the other child.

This game is fun when you use the following poem with the game:

When you send a Valentine
That's the time for fun!
Push it underneath the door,
Ring the bell and run, run, run!
Ring the bell and run!

BE MY VALENTINE

Play this game as you would play "Duck ,Duck, Grey Duck." Instead of using the words Duck and Grey Duck, have the children walk around the circle and say "Friend, Friend, Friend, Be My Valentine." The child who is touched with the words "Be My Valentine" would get up and chase the other child around the circle.

SECRET VALENTINES

It is so much fun to receive a Valentine from a Secret Friend. Assign each of the children in your class a secret Valentine. The children must make Valentines for their secret Valentine. Pass out the Valentines and see if the children can figure out who made them the Valentine.

My Valentine Story

Write a story about your best friend, a family member or someone special that you would like to have as your Valentine.

Name_____

VALENTINE'S DAY MUSIC ACTIVITIES

A VALENTINE

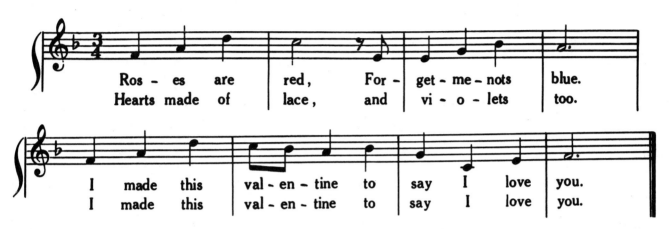

Ros - es are red, For - get - me - nots blue.
Hearts made of lace, and vi - o - lets too.

I made this val - en - tine to say I love you.
I made this val - en - tine to say I love you.

TWO VALENTINES FOR YOU

Here are Two Val - en - tines ____ For you Val - en-tines

bright and gay ____ The mess-ag-es you'll find in- side these

hearts, so red. Brings wish-es for your hap-pi - ness to - day ____

____ The lac - y frills a - round each one, Add beau-ty, and

joy and cheer ____ For Val - en - tine's the day for

thoughts of sweet - hearts thro' the year ____

VALENTINE'S DAY BULLETIN BOARD

VALENTINE'S DAY POST OFFICE

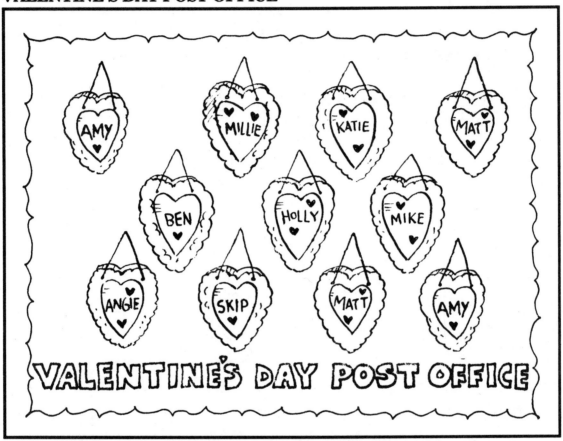

The Valentine's Day Post Office bulletin board is created by having each of the children make their own mail box. The following "mail box" idea is simple for young children to make and durable enough to last through the Valentine's Day festivities.

Cut two 8" paper plates into a heart shape. Staple the plates together, leaving the top open. Decorate with a variety of interesting materials: glitter, foil, sequins, scrap fabric, etc. Attach a string for hanging. Print the child's name on the front and hang it on the bulletin board.

SUGGESTED READING LIST

Cohen, Miriam. *"Bee My Valentine."* Greenwillow Books. Copyright © 1978. *Summary:* The students of a first grade class prepare for their St. Valentine's Day party.

Greydanus, Rose. *Valentine's Day Grump.* Troll Associates. Copyright © 1981. *Summary:* A Valentine might make Gus the Grump happy but nobody dares give him one.

Hoban, Lillian. *Arthur's Great Big Valentine.* Harper & Row. Copyright 1989. *Summary:* After they have a falling out, Arthur and his best friend Norman make up with very special Valentines.

Lexau, Joan. *Don't Be My Valentine.* Harper & Row. Copyright © 1985. *Summary:* Sam's mean Valentine for Amy Lou goes astray at school and almost ruins the day for him and his friends.

Modell, Frank. *One Zillion Valentines.* Greenwillow Books. Copyright © 1981. *Summary:* When Marvin shows Milton how to make a Valentine, they decide to make one for each person in their neighborhood.

Schultz, Gwen. *The Blue Valentine*. Morrow. Newly Illustrated Copyright © 1979. *Summary:* New to her school, Cindy strives to make contact with her teacher by sending her a Valentine in her favorite color.

Sharmat, Marjorie Weinman. *The Best Valentine in The World.* Holiday House. Copyright © 1982. *Summary:* Although Ferdinand has worked on his Valentine for Florette since November he's sure that she has forgotten him on Valentine's Day.

PRESIDENT'S DAY

CONTENTS

LET'S LEARN ABOUT ABRAHAM LINCOLN

WHO WAS ABRAHAM LINCOLN?

February 12th is an important date on our calendar. Sometimes it is printed in red. It is one of our holidays because it's the birthday of one of our greatest Presidents, Abraham Lincoln.

"Abe," as he was called, was born in a little log cabin in Kentucky. His parents were very poor. When Abe was just a boy, perhaps as big as you, he worked hard to help his family make a living in the wilderness. Food was cooked in a large kettle hung over a fire, and on cold winter days it took much wood to keep the little cabin warm.

Abe slept on a bed of leaves in the loft, which he reached by climbing a ladder. Often the snow would blow in, between the logs and on his bed.

There was not much chance for him to go to school, but his mother helped him to read books and to study. After his work was finished, he would read far into the night. Abe didn't have paper and pencils. He wrote on a wooden shovel with a piece of charcoal. The only light was from the fire in the fireplace.

He studied very hard, and when he became a young man, he was a very fine lawyer. Later he was elected to be President of the United States.

One of the most important things he did when he was President was to sign a paper called the "Emancipation Proclamation," which made all the slaves free.

Today the whole world remembers Abraham Lincoln for his kindness, his wisdom and his honesty.

ABRAHAM LINCOLN
Abraham Lincoln was honest and strong.
He served his country well and so long.

He could split many logs so all were told.
In body and mind Abe Lincoln was bold.

Pantomime scenes from Lincoln's life such as cutting logs, reading by firelight, etc. Make a beard from black construction paper. Attach to face with tape or string. After reading a story about Abraham Lincoln *(particularly his life in a log cabin)* ask the children what things they might have missed if they had lived back in the time of Abe Lincoln.

ABRAHAM LINCOLN

LET'S LEARN ABOUT
GEORGE WASHINGTON

WHO WAS GEORGE WASHINGTON?

February 22nd is the birthday of George Washington, the first President of the United States.

George Washington grew up on a fine plantation in Virginia. Here he played with his brothers and sisters and had his own pony to ride.

As George grew to be a young man, he wanted very much to help his country. At this time, our country belonged to England and when we fought a war with England to make our country free, George Washington was chosen to be Commander-In-Chief of the Army. He was such a good leader that after we won the war and became a free country, the people still wanted him to be their leader. So they elected him President of our new country.

This is why we say, "George Washington, first in war, first in peace, and first in the hearts of his countrymen."

GEORGE WASHINGTON
George Washington was our first President
Honest and strong and a very nice gent.

We'll always remember George Washington
Who fought many battles until he won.

Look for coins or dollar bills with a picture of George Washington. Read a brief story about George Washington. Ask the children what they liked about him? Talk about the story of George Washington and the Cherry Tree. *(See the rhyme, When Washington Was Only Five, found on page 130.)* Let the children sample some real cherries.

GEORGE WASHINGTON

PRESIDENT ACTIVITIES

GEORGE AND MARTHA'S DANCE

This dance should be performed to the song "Yankee Doodle." In groups three abreast, move forward in a circle around the room.

First line of song
March forward, holding hands.
Second line
Middle child swings one on outside in a little circle.
Third line
Middle child swings one on inside of circle.
Fourth line
Middle child moves forward to middle place of pair infront.
On chorus
Skip around in groups of three. Proceed around the circle.

MARCHING TO PATRIOTIC SONGS

Marching is a gross motor skill that is developed very early. Many toddlers are very good at marching. (Not only is easy, but it is also a lot of fun and good exercise!) There are many good children's records that feature patriotic songs. If you don't have one it is worth the investment. Patriotic songs are among the best marching songs. Play some good old fashioned "American" music and let your children enjoy marching to the music.

WHEN WASHINGTON WAS ONLY FIVE

When Washington was only five,
As it was told to me.
He took his shiny hatchet,
And he chopped a cherry tree.

The tree was new and very small,
Beside a bigger one.
And thoughtless George cut it down,
Because he thought it was fun.

His father walking out that day,
Was cross to find it gone.
And sternly spoke to little George,
"Come here to me, my son."

"Do you know why this little tree,
Is lying on the ground?"
"Oh yes, sir. It was I who made
My hatchet cut it down.

"How sad!" his father said to him,
And now it cannot grow.
But though you did a foolish thing,
You told the truth, I know."

(This is a fun story to tell on the flannel board. Make George, his father, a cherry tree, and a small hatchet.)

Who Is Our President Today?

Look in the newspaper and magazines to find pictures of the President of the United States.
Cut out the pictures and paste them on this paper.

Write the President's name.

_____

- -

_____

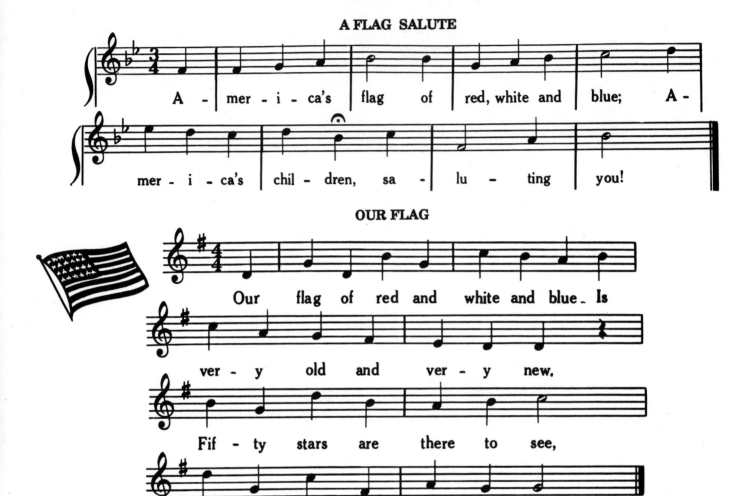

A FLAG SALUTE

A - mer - i - ca's | flag | of | red, white and | blue; | A-
mer - i - ca's | chil - dren, sa - | lu - | ting | you!

OUR FLAG

Our | flag | of | red and | white and blue. | Is
ver - y | old | and | ver - y | new.
Fif - ty | stars | are | there | to | see,
Fif - ty | states | all | proud and | free.

YANKEE DOODLE

(Read the following paragraphs and have the children learn the song "Yankee Doodle")

"Yankee Doodle" is a song that George Washington's soldiers sang as they marched up and down the countryside and into battle. The tune is an old one. A long time ago, English mothers used to sing "Yankee Doodle Doodle Down" to their children. In the war, the English sang it to make fun of George Washington's aarmy. But George Washington's soldiers liked it so much that they made it their marching song.

Do you know why we sing "And they called it macaroni?" Because in George Washington's time, the young Englishmen who dressed in fancy Italian clothes - and probably wore feathers in their hats - were called "Macaroni." So the English soldiers were still making fun of our soldiers when they called them "macaronimen." But George Washington loved this song, and we still like to sing it today.

Make a list of all the Presidents

_____   _____

_____   _____

_____   _____

_____   _____

_____   _____

_____   _____

_____   _____

_____   _____

_____   _____

_____   _____

_____   _____

_____   _____

_____   _____

_____   _____

_____   _____

_____   _____

This is an excellent small group project.

AMERICAN SYMBOLS

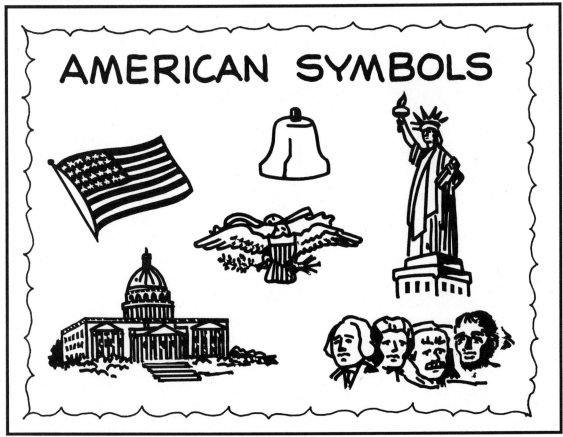

In our country we have a great many symbols that represent American history and our American freedoms, such as: the Statue of Liberty, Mount Rushmore, the Liberty Bell, the American Flag, the Bald Eagle, etc. Display these pictures for the children. Tell the children a little about each of the symbols. What do the symbols represent? What is the symbol's history? Why is the symbol important? Who made it? Who gave it to us? This may seem advanced for young children, but it is surprising how much they will remember and appreciate knowing.

PRESIDENT ACTIVITIES

WHO IS OUR PRESIDENT?

Show the children pictures of our current President. Talk about what the President does. Where the President works. Where the President lives? What does our President like to do. Who are the members of the President's family.

PATRIOTIC MOBILE

Make Uncle Sam's hat *(as shown in the illustration)*. Let the children mount pictures depicting American scenes on both sides of poster board. Suspend the pictures from the outer edge of the hat brim. This mobile provides a means of displaying U.S. historical scenes or patriotic figures.

ASSIGNING PRESIDENTS

Assign each of the children one President. Try not to choose Lincoln, Washington, or a President that many of the children already know something about. Ask the children to find out something about the President that they were assigned. You may wish to send a note home to the parents so they can assist in the research.

AMERICAN FLAGS

Provide the children with strips of red paper, an 8" x 11" sheet of white paper, a blue square and star stickers.

The children glue the red strips on the white construction paper. The blue square is then glued on the construction paper. The children can stick or lick the star stickers and place them on the blue square.

American Flag

Color the flag. Cut out the flag. Tape the flag to a straw.

SUGGESTED READING LIST

Blassingame, Wyatt. *The Look-It-Up Book of Presidents.* Random House. Copyright © 1984. *Summary:* Biographies on all the Presidents through Ronald Reagan, including photographs.

Cary, Barbara. *Meet Abraham Lincoln.* Randon House. Copyright © 1974.

Coy, Harold. *The First Book Of Presidents.* Franklin Watts. Revised Copyright © 1981. *Summary:* Discusses all the Presidents through Ronald Reagan. Includes chapters on "Who can be a President? - How is a President elected? - The White House - The President is a traveling man" - and many more.

Lee, Susan. *George Washington.* Children's Press Copyright © 1974.

Roop, Peter. *Buttons for George Washington.* Carolrhoda Books. Copyright © 1986. *Summary:* Reconstructs a possible mission of John Darragh, a 14 year old Quaker Spy who carried messages to George Washington's camp in the buttons of his coat during the Reeolutionary War.

Sloate, Susan. *Abraham Lincoln - The Freedom President.* Fawcett Columbine. Copyright © 1989. *Summary:* Profiles the life and times of Abraham Lincoln. Chapters are included on Lincoln's youth through his assassination.

TEDDY BEARS

CONTENTS

TEDDY BEAR ART ACTIVITIES

MY SPECIAL BEAR

You will need: Paper bags; black, white, and brown construction paper; glue; and markers. Cut eyes, nose, and ears. The children will glue the pieces onto the paper bag. The bear's mouth may be added with a black marker.

The children may wish to use their puppets to dramatize the story of *The Three Bears* or another favorite bear story.

LIFE-SIZE BEARS

Using very large white paper, have the child lie down on the paper. The teacher or another child should trace around the child's body. When tracing, keep the pencil or marker at least two inches from the child's body. The objective is to have the child's body look wider and heavier. The children are to color their drawings to look like bears. Display the life-size bears up and down the halls of your school.

POPSICLE STICK BEAR PUPPETS

It is easy to locate teddy bear stickers. You will be able to find them at greeting card stores, school supply stores, and probably in your local drug stores. Have the children put the stickers on the top of a popsicle stick or a tongue depressor. These make wonderful "little" stick puppets. The children can decorate a shoe box and use that as a puppet stage for their stick puppets.

PAPER PLATE BEARS

Have the children paint a paper plate brown. *(The heavy paper plates work best.)* When the paint is dry, the children can add brown construction paper ears and other construction paper facial features. Add a bow tie or a hair ribbon on the bear.

TEDDY BEAR LANGUAGE ACTIVITIES

THE TRAVELING TEDDY BEAR

The Traveling Teddy Bear is a delightful experience for children, but will call for some help from the children's parents. The teacher should bring a teddy bear to school. *(I would guess that all teachers have a teddy bear somewhere in their homes!)* Name this bear and introduce him to the children in your classroom. Explain to the children that this bear loves to travel and spend the night in the homes of children. He has come to our school so he *(or she)* can have a turn spending the night at each of your homes. Doesn't that sound fun?

Each child will have a turn taking the bear home for the night. *(Children take this responsibility very seriously!)* The next morning when the child brings the bear back to school, the child should make an oral report to the class about all the fun things that the bear did at their house. What games did the bear play with you? Did the bear get a good nights sleep? Where did the bear sleep? Did the other people in your house like the bear? It is so much fun to listen to the stories that children are able to create about their very special overnight guest.

When preparing for this activity, send a note home to the parents describing the activity. Encourage the parents to help their child take responsibility for this guest. In other words help the parents to play along with you.

I would also advise that the bear stay at school over the weekend. Having the responsibility of the bear for two nights and three days is overwhelming, not to mention that it is not fair that only a few children would have a weekend turn.

BUILD-A-BEAR

Pre-cut the parts of a large bear from brown grocery bags. The larger you make the body parts, the more successful this experience will be.

Begin by taping the bear's middle *(stomach)* section to the wall. Tell the children that they will have to help you build the bear. Bears are very large and far too much work for just one person. Ask the children what parts of the bear are missing. As the children are able to name the body parts, tape those parts onto the bear. When you are finished, you will have created a darling wall display, and the children will have had an educational experience in naming body parts and in observing missing parts. *(Older children may wish to work in groups of 4 and create their own bears.)*

TEDDY BEAR LANGUAGE ACTIVITIES

TEDDY BEAR DAY

Most children have a special teddy bear or stuffed animal. *(Yes, even those very grown-up second graders still have a special stuffed animal.)* Ask each of the children to bring their special animal to school. Be sure to explain that the children do not have to bring a teddy bear. The children may bring any stuffed animal that is important to them.

When all the children have brought their special animal to school have a sharing time. Ask the children to introduce their animal to the class. What is the animal's name? Who gave the child the animal? Where does the animal sleep at night? What does the animal like to play with? Does their stuffed animal eat anything? Where are some of the places that they have taken their stuffed animal? Encourage good expressive, creative language skills.

Have the children draw pictures of their special stuffed animal. Display these pictures in the classroom. Older children may wish to write about their stuffed animal. "Why is the stuffed animal so important to the me?"

GOLDILOCKS AND THE THREE BEARS

Children love the story of *Goldilocks and the Three Bears*. Using the puppets your class has made from the *art activities found on page 140,* have the children re-tell the story of *Goldilocks and the Three Bears.*

Ask the children to dramatize the story of *Goldilocks and the Three Bears*. Divide your class into groups. Have each group practise their skit and then present it to the class or possibly present their production to another classroom in your school building.

Think up new endings for the story. What are some other ways that this story could have ended? Could Goldilock's parents have come to the Bear's cottage? Could Baby Bear have walked Goldilocks home? Children often think up some very creative endings.

LOOK AT MY TEDDY BEAR

Color the bear with your favorite colors.

Name _____

TEDDY BEAR MOVEMENT GAMES

BEAR HUNTING

Cut a tagboard bear and staple it on a two-inch piece of string. The class chooses one child to hide the bear, while they sit with their eyes closed. (No peeking!) The bear may be completely covered but the string must be left showing.

The children get up and search for the bear. The searchers do not touch the bear or exclaim when they have spotted the bear. The children shuld go back quietly and sit in their places. In this way, each child must find the bear. The first child back in place will be the next to hide the bear.

BIG BROWN BEAR

Read the following poem to the class:
Big Brown Bear
Will you dance for me?
That is what I'd like to see!

Have the children dramatize the movements of a bear. Who can look the most like a dancing bear? Do bears move slowly? Do bears move fast?

This is also an excellent poem for beginning readers. Have the children copy the poem and then draw an illustration to accompnay the poem.

HIDE THE BEAR

The teacher hides a toy bear somewhere in the classroom. One child at a time tries to locate the bear by listening to the teacher's verbal directions such as; far ... farther ... on your right ... turn left ... near ... nearer...etc. The children will have fun searching for the bear and the children will also be developing a greater understanding of following directions and of positional concepts.

TEDDY BEAR LEARNING ACTIVITIES

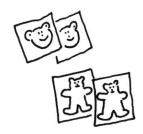

TEDDY BEAR MATCH-UP

This activity can be made by either cutting out pictures of bears or teddy bears from magazines, or the teacher may wish to draw pictures of bears. Make two identical sets of bears. Glue the pictures of the bears on tagboard squares. *(You may wish to laminate the pictures for lasting durability.)* Have the children match the pictures of the bears that are identical.

Version Two: Draw pictures of bear faces on the tagboard squares. Make pairs of happy bears, sad bears, angry bears, etc.

TEDDY BEAR COOKIES

You will need: 1 and 1/2 cups soft butter; 2 eggs; 4 teaspoons baking powder; 5 cups flour; 2 cups sugar; 1 teaspoon salt; 1/2 cup milk; 1 teaspoon vanilla.

Cream butter and sugar. Add eggs and beat until fluffy. Siff together dry ingredients and add with milk and vanilla to egg mixture. Chill well. Children may shape cookies or use cookie cutters. Bake at 375° degrees for eight minutes. Makes 100 cookies. The children may decorate as desired.

IDENTIFY BEAR VOICES

Read the story of "The Three Bears," using different pitches of your voice to represent the three different bears. After reading the selection, speak in the voice of one of the bears and ask the children to identify the character. Let the children take turns speaking in the bear's voices.

WHAT DO BEARS EAT?

Most bears will eat practically anything. But bears who live in the forest like to hunt for berries. Plan a snack for the children of various kinds of berries. Besides are the usual kinds of berries (strawberries, raspberries, blueberries) bring in some types of berries that the children may not have experienced (gooseberries, cranberries, and the berries from inside a pomagranite). What fun new taste sensations! How many of the children think that they could be bears and eat berries all the time?

THE THREE BEARS

(Melody:"The Ants Go Marching One By One")

Oh, here is Great Big **Papa Bear** - uh-huh, uh-huh   *(put up Papa Bear)*
And here is Medium-Size **Mama Bear** - uh-huh, uh-huh   *(put up Mama Bear)*
And here is little **Baby Bear**; he's the one with the fuzzy hair *(put up Baby Bear)*
And they all lived in the woods: deep in the woods
Deep in the woods - hmm, hmm, hmm.

Well, Papa Bear - he likes to build - uh-huh, uh-huh   *(put up saw)*
And Mama Bear - she likes to cook - uh-huh, uh-huh *(put up mixing bowl with spoon)*
And Baby Bear - he likes to play; he plays ball outside all day   *(put up ball/bat)*
And they all lived in the woods: deep in the woods
Deep in the woods - hmm, hmm, hmm.

A little girl named **Goldilocks** - uh-huh, uh-huh   *(put up Goldilocks)*
Went knocking on the three bears door - uh-huh, uh-huh   *(put up house)*
She walked into their house that day;
No one was there - they had gone a-way
They went walk-ing in the woods: deep in the woods
Deep in the woods - hmm, hmm, hmm.

The bears came back and found a mess, - uh-huh, uh-huh   *(put up chair/bowl)*
An empty bowl, a broken chair, - uh-huh, uh-huh   *(point to bowl; point to chair)*
They went upstairs to baby bear's bed
Goldilocks screamed and bumped her head!   *(put up Goldilocks in bed)*
And she ran a-way from the bears - deep in the woods
Deep in the woods, deep in the woods!   *(sung slower)*

Additional Activity Ideas

1. *Rhythm:* This song is excellent for clapping hands, slapping thighs, tapping chest, stomping feet, and striking rhythm instruments.

2. *Language:* Use the flannel board figures as stick puppets. Attach a small piece of the soft part of the velcro to the back of Goldilocks and each of the three bears. Glue a small piece of the rougher part of the velcro onto tongue depressor sticks. Attach the cut out characters onto the sticks by means of the velcro. Have four children hold up the appropriate character as the song is sung by the class.

3. *Dramatization:* Have children act out the parts of the four characters with the appropriate actions as the song is sung.

From Songs for the Flannel Board,
by Connie Walters and Diane Totten.
Copyright © T.S. Denison & Co., Inc.

Patterns found on page 147.

TEDDY BEAR MUSIC PATTERNS

Patterns for the song, "The Three Bears" found on page 146.

TEDDY BEAR BULLETIN BOARDS

TEDDY BEAR PARADE

Children love to look through old catalogs and cut out all the pictures. Have the children search through old magazines and catalogs to find pictures of bears. Have the children cut-out all the bears they can find.

Back the bulletin board with white paper. Let the children draw on the paper to create a forest scene. When the children have finished drawing and coloring the forest, the children can add all the bears that were cut out of the magazines.

TEDDY BEAR BULLETIN BOARDS

TEDDY BEAR STORIES

This bulletin board should be prepared on the first day that you plan to begin the Teddy Bear unit. The Teddy Bear Stories bulletin board will grow and deveop as you move through the Teddy Bear unit. Each day of the Teddy Bear unit read a story to your class about a bear or teddy bear. There are many famous bears; Winnie-the-Pooh, Corduroy, Smokey the Bea,; the Three Bears, the Berenstain Bears, etc. Everyday after you have read a bear story, put the jacket of the book or a drawing of the story's main bear character on the bulletin board.

The children will enjoy seeing all the bears they have heard about in the stories. On ocassion review the names of the bears on the bulletin board and see if the children can retell some of the stories.

TEDDY BEAR RHYMES/POETRY

MY TEDDY BEAR

My Teddy Bear,
    Sleeps with me at night.   *(pretend to sleep)*
My Teddy Bear,
    I always hold tight.   *(pretend to give hug)*
My Teddy Bear,
    Can roll on the rug.   *(roll)*
My Teddy Bear,
    Gives great big hugs!   *(pretend to give great big hug)*

I'M YOUR LITTLE STUFFED BEAR
(Sung to the tune of "I'm A Little Teapot")

I'm you little stuffed bear
    Please hug me.
See my eyes twinkle,
    I'm so happy.

When the night time comes,
    I'll sleep with you.
Just tuck me in,
    And I'll kiss you!

CAN YOU?

Read the following rhyme to the children. Have the children pantomime the movements as you read the rhyme:

Can you hop like a rabbit?
Can you jump like a frog?
Can you walk like a duck?
Can you run like a dog?

Can you fly like a bird?
Can you swim like a fish?
Can you sleep like a bear?
Be as still as you wish.

LITTLE FURRY TEDDY BEAR

Pretend you are teddy bears waiting in a store for someone to buy you. How would you sit? What expression would you have on your face? Someone will come along and buy you and take you to their seat. *(Let the children take turns being the teddy bear and being the child who buys the teddy bear.)*

Little furry teddy bear,
You look so quiet sitting there.
With your brown and shaggy hair,
Resting still upon your chair,
You look so quiet sitting there.

From Quiet Times, by Louise Binder Scott. Copyright © T.S. Denison & Co., Inc.

Suggested Reading List

Freeman, Don. **Beady Bear.** Viking Copyright © 1954. *Summary:* A toy bear goes off to a cave to live as a real bear should, only to find he needs something more to be truly happy.

Freeman, Don. **Corduroy.** Viking. Copyright © 1968. *Summary:* A toy bear in a department store wants a number of things, but when a little girl finally buys him he finds what he has wanted most of all.

Maris, Ron. **Are You There, Bear?** Greenwillow Books. Copyright © 1984. *Summary:* In a darkened bedroom, several toys search for a teddy bear finally finding him reading a book behind a chair.

Milne, A.A. **Winnie-The-Pooh.** Gyandzhlik. Copyright © 1984. *Summary:* The classic story of a teddy bear, his human friend Christopher Robin and other memorable animals including Piglet and Eeyore.

Stevenson, James. **The Night After Christmas.** Greenwillow Books. Copyright © 1981. *Summary:* Tossed in garbage cans after they are replaced by new toys at Christmas a teddy bear and a doll are befriended by a stray dog.

Waber, Bernard. **Ira Sleeps Over.** Houghton. Copyright © 1972. *Summary:* A little boy is excited at the prospect of spending the night at his friends house - but worries how he'll get along without his teddy bear.

Wahl, Jan. **Humphrey's Bear.** Holt, Rinehart & WInston. Copyright © 1987. *Summary:* Humphrey has wonderful adventures with his toy bear after they go to bed at night, just as his father did before him.

DECEMBER

Sunday	Monday	Tuesday	Wednesday	Thursday	Friday	Saturday

T.S. Denison & Co., Inc.

152

Totally Winter

JANUARY

Sunday	Monday	Tuesday	Wednesday	Thursday	Friday	Saturday

T.S. Denison & Co., Inc.

Totally Winter

FEBRUARY

Sunday	Monday	Tuesday	Wednesday	Thursday	Friday	Saturday

DEC EM BER

F E B
R U
A R Y

WINTER ANNOUNCEMENTS!

To _____ **Date** _____

_____

_____

_____

_____

_____

_____

_____

_____

_____

_____

_____

_____

TEACHER

TEACHER NOTES